Creating the Special World

Creating the Special World

A Collection of Lectures
by
Weston H. Noble

Edited by Steven M. Demorest

With a Foreword by Paul Salamunovich

GIA Publications, Inc.
Chicago

G–6529
© 2005 GIA Publications, Inc.
7404 S. Mason Ave., Chicago, IL 60638
www.giamusic.com
ISBN: 1-57999-515-2
Book layout: Paul Burrucker

Printed in the United States of America.

Contents

Editor's Preface

When Mr. Noble asked if I would edit his lectures for publication, I was very excited to have an opportunity to give something back to a teacher who had given so much to me. My experience echoes that of so many others. As a high school student, I had the opportunity to sing with Mr. Noble both at the Dorian Music Camp and in a local performance of the Brahms *Requiem*. These experiences, along with those in my high school choir, led me to attend Luther College and pursue choral music as my life's work.

Through the process of working on these talks and meeting with Mr. Noble, it became clear to me, once again, that I was receiving much more than I was giving. After twenty plus years, it was exciting to revisit some of the ideas I first encountered as a singer in the Nordic Choir and as a student in choral methods class. I find them just as insightful and inspiring today as they were then, perhaps more so as I view them from the perspective of an experienced teacher and educator of teachers. I believe that the ideas have remained fresh because Mr. Noble himself has never stopped being a student. As these lectures demonstrate, he is constantly looking for new ideas and new insights into the choral art that he can incorporate into his teaching.

The lectures in this volume were given in various forms over many years and were never intended as a set.

For that reason, you will notice certain ideas may be repeated in different lectures because that particular audience may not have heard the other lecture. Nine of the lectures fall into three general topics: **The Special World of Choral Music, Choral Pedagogy,** and **Stylistic Awareness.**

The first section, **The Special World of Choral Music,** contains three lectures that focus on an area Mr. Noble has emphasized more than any other conductor or teacher I know: our role in touching students' lives and striving for a higher spiritual plane. All of the subsequent lectures in the collection, which are more technical in nature, must be understood as starting from the perspective of elevating the human spirit through music.

The four lectures under **Choral Pedagogy** deal with more "nuts and bolts" aspects of choral teaching and artistry. While it may be difficult to get the complete flavor of these lectures in their written form, I believe the reader will find important insights for the teaching conductor. The two lectures on **Stylistic Awareness** should be read with the understanding that many of the ideas were first presented in the late 1950s and early 1960s. These talks include musical examples to illustrate the points being made.

The final lecture is a very personal overview of the history of *a cappella* choral singing in the United States from the last century to the present. It is fascinating in that it includes eyewitness (or "ear-witness") accounts of hearing many of the giants of the field in live performances. To read the history of choral singing from the standpoint of someone who first observed, then participated, and eventually led our profession is a unique experience.

This collection represents only a small portion of the numerous lectures and clinics Mr. Noble has given over his long career. I hope that you will enjoy, as I have, this

5

chance to study and reflect on the insights of one of the most influential choral conductors and teachers our country has ever known.

Thank you, Mr. Noble, for introducing me to that special world.

– Steven M. Demorest

Steven M. Demorest *is Associate Professor of Choral Music Education and chairman of the Music Education division at the University of Washington. He is the author of* Building Choral Excellence: Teaching Sight-singing in the Choral Rehearsal, *published by Oxford University Press. Demorest holds a Ph.D. from the University of Wisconsin-Madison, a master of music from Westminster Choir College, and a bachelor of arts from Luther College, where he sang in the Nordic Choir.*

Foreword

I am very pleased to be writing an introduction for this collection of lectures by Weston Noble. It is gratifying to see these talks, given over so many years in professional situations, being made available to a larger audience.

I first met Weston more than forty-five years ago in Los Angeles, California, when he was there as a guest of Roger Wagner at a recording session of Wagner's Chorale at Capitol Records. We hit it off immediately. Since that time we have shared the stage at numerous clinics and conferences, and I have always admired Weston's ability to translate his artistry into clear and compelling language. Even in discussing the more technical aspects, he never loses sight of the ultimate goal: to change lives through the power of music.

We have had many long talks over the years about choral style and the importance of spirituality in making music. Weston is an intensely spiritual person, and in that vein I found we were kindred spirits. When he brought his Nordic Choir to Los Angeles to record at Capitol Records, I was fortunate to be in the recording booth as his "ears." I still remember the tonal and spiritual beauty of the choir's singing and their gorgeous ensemble quality. I have had the pleasure of having former Nordic Choir members as singers in some of my groups, and they reflect the dedication and spiritual approach to music making they learned from him.

The depth of Weston Noble's impact on our profession is widespread. He has guest conducted at more than 750 music festivals nationally and internationally, and his Luther College Nordic Choir has performed in most of the major concert halls. His numerous honors, including Outstanding United States Music Educator and the ACDA's Robert Lawson Shaw Citation, are clear testaments to his role as a leader in the field of choral music. Many of the students he taught during his fifty-six years at Luther College and those he has touched through his numerous clinics and workshops have gone on to make beautiful music in churches, schools, and communities all over the world. His most enduring legacy is the life-changing impact he had on the singers who had the good fortune to work with him. Thousands, young and old, have been touched by Weston Noble through an All-State or Festival clinic, and still remember their encounter with the special world of choral music. By becoming a servant of the music, he demonstrates that conductors can allow music to speak through them clearly and purely.

I hope that through reading his lectures you may truly appreciate the character, warmth, tremendous wisdom, and dedication of Weston H. Noble.

– Paul Salamunovich

Paul Salamunovich *is Director of Music at St. Charles Borromeo Church in North Hollywood, a position he has held since 1949. He was also Director of Choral Activities at Mount St. Mary's College for eighteen years and Loyola Marymount University for twenty-seven years, leaving the university in 1991 to* *become Music Director of the Los Angeles Master Chorale. In April 2001, he was named Music Director Emeritus of the Chorale. Salamunovich has conducted almost one thousand clinics and festivals throughout the world and has been responsible for choral music in numerous motion pictures and television productions. He has also been knighted by the Vatican for his contributions in the field of sacred music.*

The Special World
of Choral Music

Lecture 1
Bring the Special World into Reality

> Any great work of art is great because it creates a special world of its own. It revives and readapts time and space, and the measure of its success is the extent to which it invites you in and lets you breathe its strange, special air.
>
> – Leonard Bernstein

May I share a letter I received from a student who attended our Dorian Music Camp at Luther College?

> During my week at Luther, I experienced a **wonderful** sensation whenever the choir broke into song! The whole room seemed to burst forth with emotion! What a change from our high school choir! I have never considered myself to have amazing vocal talent, but even so at the Grand Concert I put my heart into all of the songs that were performed! Your choir room is an experience I'll never forget! And I am positive I'll always remember the words and the emotions for all of my Dorian songs!

What happened to this girl? What did she experience that truly transformed those hours? Her sense of time and space were transformed. It was sheer joy for her. She

13

was truly in a **special** world, one she hated to leave. She became completely open as she poured forth her heart at the final concert. It would be an understatement to say she experienced something powerful, something she will desire to seek again and again. It is not dramatic to say her life will never be the same. It will always contain a new realization, and with that a new search.

Is that why you are here today? Are you still searching without consciously knowing it? It is obvious you are here for a renewed inspiration, new choral techniques, new repertoire, but maybe you had an experience at one time similar to this young lady's. Maybe you still desire to relive such moments, and, yes, even to "create" such experiences for others. I had such a moment as this young lady; it is the reason I am here today!

When I was a junior in high school, I played solo-chair clarinet in a band that received a Division III rating at contest. The Monday following the contest, the director said we were going to begin rehearsing next year's contest selection that very day and thereby receive a Division I the following year. I was excited!

"Take out *Light Calvary Overture* of Von Suppe," he said. We began to sight read this overture. As I was struggling with the sixteenth notes, the cornets entered with a fanfare-like theme. What hit me? My backbone rippled with excitement; I felt totally alive for a brief moment. It was so special, so much so I still recall every detail with great pleasure. Can you relate to this? Of course you can!

Let us look at my experience in greater detail. Were we good? No. In addition, we were sight reading. Was I an outstanding player? No. Did the young lady who wrote me the note consider herself an outstanding singer? No. Yet it happened to both of us! We entered a special world, no matter how briefly, and we will never forget it. I was fourteen at the time. I know a

14

former Luther student who experienced this in second grade when the high school choir visited her class. She was not an active participant, not at all schooled in the art of music. This "special world" can be experienced anywhere, anytime. Is this not encouraging?

What is this special feeling we experienced? What happened within us to produce such an unforgettable moment? In all of my reading, I have never found an explanation of this phenomenon. May I share my personal theory? To do so, I must review who we are as individuals.

Look at 1 Thessalonians 5:23: "I pray God your whole **spirit, soul** and **body** be preserved blameless unto the coming of our Lord Jesus Christ." We are tri-partite in nature, spirit, soul, and body. Our body receives impressions, the information that comes in from the physical world. Impressions come through the senses. Our senses link us to the earth and thereby create and maintain contact with the world around us. This is our **outer self**, the source of surface self-love, what we sense about ourselves. Our soul is our psychological part that is also tri-partite in nature: the mind, will, and emotions. These three comprise the ego, the center of our personality, the **inner self**. (Notice I am using the Greek definition of the word "soul" and not the Hebrew.)

Our spirit is that part of us that allows us to reach outside ourselves, beyond our soul and body. In Genesis we read that God breathed spirit into matter and "humankind became a living soul." The three parts are matter, soul, spirit—or body, psychological dimension, and spiritual dimension. Our Spirit was made in God's image so we can respond to Him—our Spirit is His link for guidance and instruction.

Confusion can exist between the soul and spirit. Mary, in the *Magnificat*, said: "My **soul** doth magnify the Lord and my **spirit** hath rejoiced in God my Savior."

15

Hebrews 4:12 states: "For the word of God is living and powerful, and sharper than any two-edged sword, piercing even to the division of soul and spirit."

There is a hierarchy and function in our tri-partite nature. The above diagram depicts the hierarchy. In day-to-day experiences, it might seem the body is number one in importance. In actuality, however, it is the least important at number three. Notice our soul is more important than our body, but, again, it is not number one. Our spirit transcends everything. It alone is number one. That does not mean that in everyday life it always comes first. More often than not it does not. But it should! What is the first thing you thought of this morning upon awakening? I'm tired? I need coffee? What should I wear? Maybe you thought of your emotional state (your soul). For most it was anything but the spirit. To correct this misalignment in my life, I have disciplined myself to say upon awakening: "The stead-fast love of the Lord never ceases. His mercies never come to an end. They are new every morning. Great is thy faithfulness." (Lamentations 3:22–23)

Let us examine the functions of our tri-partite nature. Having established that the spirit is number one, it thus functions to **inspire** the soul. Its role is to animate the mind, the will, and our emotions—those times when life has its greatest meaning. The soul, in turn, functions to **rule** the body. Proof? Psychosomatic medicine! The body can directly reflect our emotional state—positive or negative.

When we reach out beyond ourselves, we feed our spirit (e.g., Egyptians and the pyramids, the Greeks and the temples, the Indians and the "great spirit"). Every civilization has had its own manner of reaching out for something greater than their earthly existence. When we reach out through our faith, particularly Christianity, I use a capital "S"—Spirit. When we reach out in other ways, I use a small "s"—spirit. Anything aesthetic in nature feeds our human spirit, most certainly the arts.

We need to feed all three areas. We obviously feed our bodies daily as well as our minds, especially as students and teachers. Emotions are such a large part of daily life, with our senses being a strong vehicle for them. We employ our wills successfully or unsuccessfully every day. Sometimes we get confused as to which area needs sustenance. We may need to feed a certain emotion, but end up eating instead. Too much reliance on our mind, and we become stale. Let our emotions take over without parameters and we are in real trouble. We may feed our minds when really it is the spirit that needs feeding. (See why I stay at Luther!)

It may be viewed also in this manner. How often the triangle works in a totally opposite manner with the body and senses coming first. The mind takes over and says, "I'll figure it out. I'll think my way through." The will might take over and we tell ourselves, "If I can just try a little harder, keep the rules, make the effort." The emotions take over and say, "Whatever makes you feel good—do." **None of these three elements of the soul really knows where it is going ultimately without guidance—that being inspiration from the spirit!**

Let us go back to our discussion of the nature of our musical experience, that moment when, through the arts, the "special world" was experienced. I can now present my theory with a greater degree of understanding. I like to express those special times as moments of **wholeness** when all the disparate parts within us come together. We are for a moment non-fragmented, "all together," beautifully whole. In other words it is a moment of wholeness—something we strive for almost every moment of our lives—to feel complete. How do the arts and especially music do this? Perhaps one of the elements of music, be it the rhythm, the timbre (for me the brass), the harmony, or the melody, touches our spirit in an unusually special way. Our spirit then inspires our soul, most likely the emotions (although craftsmanship could certainly inspire the mind) and the soul, in turn, rules the body. The body reacts with tears, chills, goose bumps, a rush of joy up the back—whatever it is for that particular individual. **Everything is in line—we are momentarily whole—it is an unforgettable moment.** Though these moments are brief, we often experience a glow, a warmth that continues for a time. Yet in due course these moments disappear from our conscious reality, but only from the conscious.

What a gift we give to our students if we give them but one moment of wholeness they will remember in the course of their four years. If we give them one a year—phenomenal. In conclusion, remember this—it does not have to be a Brahms *Requiem* to produce that "special moment." I was playing in a Division III band, not the greatest player, and sight reading with the conductor not radiating an overly positive self-image. And yet my backbone went crazy. Indeed, the "special world" became a reality for me that I still recall some sixty years later!

Lecture 2
Music and the Human Spirit

Music is the voice of the spirit
                    – Robert Shaw

In 1958, at the New York Philharmonic's Young
People's Concerts, Leonard Bernstein said, "There's no
limit to the different kinds of feelings music can make
you have...every once in a while we have feelings so deep
and so special that we have no words for them and that's
where music is so marvelous; because music names them
for us, only in notes instead of words."

What a wonderful explanation of the role of music in
the realm of our human spirit. It becomes so clear what
Bernstein's quotation truly means—"no words for
them"—truly out of the area of the soul! How blessed
we are to feed our spirits daily and thereby on rare occa-
sions to have it become the vehicle for a moment of
wholeness when our spirit, soul, and body are lined up
as one. This special world experience is available to
everyone, not just students of the art of music.

Our *Messiah* chorus at Luther numbers between 800
and 900 students. One year, the captain of the football
team grabbed me after the performance and exclaimed:
"What happened to me during the 'Amen' chorus?

Never have I felt this way in my life, not even when making a touchdown!" His life was changed. He will participate in every *Messiah* performance in the future, hoping for such a sensation again! If it reoccurs, it undoubtedly will not have the same intensity, but he has been permanently changed. How? We have millions of individual brain cells. Certain experiences in life have the power to cause certain cells to form powerful connections. Most daily experiences do not have this magnetic power within our brain. Unforgettable ones, however, be they positive or negative, do have the ability to restructure our brain permanently. A musical experience is one of them! What seemed a brief, beautiful experience actually became a permanent one. Everyone has a reason to covet these moments of wholeness!

Do we underestimate the likelihood of this happening in our music groups? Is it possible for grade school and junior high students to experience this? Remember the lowly circumstance I described when I had my first music experience? It doesn't have to be the Brahms *Requiem* performed by Robert Shaw!

Our lives may have been lived more on the objective, conscious level, with us responding primarily to our day's activities and the people around us. Once we become aware that such a response can be evoked within us, a whole new search may be initiated. It may be the "fountain of youth" of our life! One wonders if those in our society who have not been in contact with the arts, and especially music, realize they have the potential within themselves for such a beautiful experience. To go through life and not to have realized this would be tragic!

To have one's life changed by a musical experience could be reason enough to covet these moments of wholeness. May I suggest that its effect might continue in another unseen way—that it might even grow within us

—that this experience could be a vital cog in the development of a more mature, healthy emotional life? Enter the word **vulnerability**.

Each one of us desires to express our inner thoughts, our inner emotions, in other words, to be vulnerable. Yet this is not an easy step to take. To say "this is me, this is who I am" takes far more courage than most of us possess. In music, this expression can take place in a non-threatening way. Howard Swan, the great choral giant, expressed it so well. He suggested that when we experience a meaningful moment in a rehearsal or concert, we really are saying to those around us or to the audience, "This is who I am. Let me share this beautiful moment with you!" Is this not what the young lady did as she "put her heart into all the songs?" At this moment we are beautifully uninhibited, for the person on each side of us protects us. They are our "Linus blankets," if you will. We are vulnerable without being exposed. We have made a deep statement about "who we are" without being threatened!

Can we seek this freedom in greater personal, individual depth as well? I have noticed that the greater our concerts on tour with the Luther Choir, the more sharing that takes place between roommates following the concert. Once we return to campus, the greater the depth of the students' vulnerability with me, as they share concerns they feel are too personal to be discussed even with the campus pastor!

What a vital step this is! We are allowing a side of us, too often repressed, to be expressed, to be brought into the realm of consciousness. We are beginning to be in touch with the "shadow side" of us, that part of us we want to keep secret. And this connection is mandatory for emotional health! The musical moment of wholeness has planted a seed within our inner person that, if nurtured, can produce lasting results. A "new life" can begin, a life that contains a full circle of lasting whole-ness rather than a single moment of initial wholeness. All of this stemming from the beauty of a shared experience through music! It is rather overwhelming. As the deepest part of our beautiful inner being can be expressed through the "special world" with its "strange, special air," so, conversely, the deepest part of our not-so-beautiful inner being now can be shared! If we deny the expression of our shadow side, we risk having our life energies dry up. John Sanford addresses this danger in his book *The Shadow Side of Reality.*

> There are times when we must allow some of the unlived life within us to live if we are to get new energies for living…The important thing, as has been said before but what must be said again for emphasis, is that we recognize the Shadow side of ourselves. This recognition alone produces a powerful and beneficial change in consciousness….everything in the unconscious that has been repressed strives for reunion with consciousness. It is as though we put certain things in the basement of our house and shut the door tightly. But these things do not want to remain in the basement. They turn into devils and rattle the door and seek to find some way out of their imprisoned state and back into the world of consciousness. In so doing, they create anxiety, since we tend to fear the return of the repressed. But this attempt of repressed contents to reach consciousness is not simply an attempt to disturb consciousness or gain revenge. The movement is toward the light of consciousness because this is necessary if psychological redemption is to occur. No matter how malignant these split-off contents of the psyche may appear to be, and no matter how malicious their tricks, there is always the possibility of their redemption if they can reach consciousness. Paradoxically, the redemption of these lost parts of ourselves also results in our redemption. That is, we

can be whole only when we have helped redeem our devils....Wholeness can only emerge when both sides of the coin are represented in consciousness at the same time, when we remain conscious of both our light and dark sides. (John Sanford. New York: Crossroads Publishing, pp. 65, 124–125)

Think of life as a lake that is calm and peaceful. A storm comes along, stirring up the bottom of the lake—the mud, the sediments, and these unwelcome elements come to the surface. There is no way this can be prevented until it is calm and peaceful again. You are in rehearsal and a stressful situation comes up. Suddenly you say something confrontational. Later you wish you had exercised more self-control. Do not regret this, for there is no way you could have had control of that moment. The malicious trick Sanford mentions has taken place and you are revealed. How can this shadow side of the psyche be redeemed? Certainly not by repression once again, but by being vulnerable—open to someone else. This split-off content must be represented in consciousness at the same time, and then healing can take place.

Another common situation for conductors can illustrate this point. Conductors are often very sensitive to the expressions on the faces of members of the organization as they are singing. Some faces seemingly reflect optimism and engagement; others seem to reflect negativism and boredom. We move on to the next face to find engagement again. A seemingly negative face when encountered too often can produce a "shadow moment." The answer—the courage of vulnerability. You must be aware that you are responding to that negative face personally without necessarily understanding the student's needs. I have found that often the facial expression I perceived as negative was just the normal expression of that student. The need to repress my reaction is gone. If the student *is* feeling negative or uninvolved, it is better to seek the reason before a "shadow encounter."

In one's personal life, one might wish to be vulnerable but be unable to find the courage to proceed. To be vulnerable with just anyone is wrong and can be very harmful. Pray that you will find that perfect person with whom to share. The result will be total acceptance by that individual, and so often that person has the right answer for you. Also, that person will end up loving you even more because of your openness. God's plan is truly beautiful!

I also found it most encouraging when I became aware that there is gold under the shadow, the gold being the "original you" before life presented its negative factors. It is highly desirable, therefore, to confront the shadow, turn the negative forces into positive ones, and let the former darkness not absorb, but reflect the gold!

Music teachers often have a strong "feeling function," the ability to respond directly to the beautiful and the not so beautiful in life. Consequently, a negative encounter can result in a shadow encounter. The propensity for shadow density is more prevalent with members of our profession. As Bernstein said, "If the heart is not free, the baton is not free." With this risk comes reward; however, the opportunities for vulnerability are also more available—what an interesting paradox!

These are powerful statements. Too powerful to be associated with music? Not in the least if the new life begun in the inner person through a musical experience is encouraged to grow. The strength of its initial beauty is such that it has the power to foster vulnerability and its ultimate rewards. This is life changing! Music, and by extension the music teacher, have become vital elements in the progress of an individual toward the realization of honesty, wholeness, and becoming a real person!

The more frequently we experience a moment of wholeness through music, the more this new life is encouraged to grow within, watered by such beauty, if you will. Our ability to love increases. And everyone knows the deep healing power of love. An unbeatable cycle has been set in motion.

Certainly none of us would do anything to inhibit the frequency of these moments of wholeness, the importance of which we have come to see so clearly. We would choose not to inhibit them, but do we? I'm afraid the answer is "yes." What did I discover I was doing to inhibit this miracle of wholeness in a rehearsal, or even in a performance? The first destructive factor present was negativism. It is impossible for a negative element to produce a positive one, and, surprisingly, we all are prone to be negative. I remember seeing on the *Today Show* the results of a study regarding our normal thought patterns. The results were alarming! The average person thinks negatively **95 percent** of the time. And those fortunate enough to work in exceptionally positive surroundings still think negatively over 75 percent of the time. No wonder we sometimes seem to obliterate this "special world" so quickly!

Why this unusually high percentage of negative thoughts? The subconscious mind, the inner person if you will, is the greatest computer ever devised. It not only records but also holds in a memory bank **every** experience of life. This includes life before birth, to wit, John the Baptist. Some say our memory goes back to conception, a startling possibility.

If this human computer is recording primarily negative thinking brought about by daily circumstances often (but not always) beyond our control, and if my unconscious constantly colors the way my conscious mind perceives daily experiences, the results are obvious. What a challenge to attack negative thinking not only in rehearsals but during the rest of the day as well! The second destructive factor is being judgmental, which is actually a source of negativism. Every time I was judgmental, I ran the risk of being negative. "How dare he be tardy to my rehearsal!" "How dare she miss this performance!" It is disheartening at times to listen to the general tone of conversation about students by faculty in the faculty lounges of our schools. Then they walk out and teach that student! We are **never** given the right to judge. "Judge not that ye be not judged!" That is a statement with no qualifications.

John Sanford differentiates between judging and evaluating when he writes,

> But this does not mean we should not evaluate other people. Judgment is different from evaluating because judgment is final....Evaluating another person can rest upon an objective appraisal of another person's character or personality. Judging another person rests upon our own unconsciousness, and this is why Jesus condemns it. (John Sanford, *Thy Kingdom Within*, Paulist Press, p. 122)

If we directors strive to enhance the frequency of musical experiences within our rehearsals by confronting our negative and judgmental thoughts outside the rehearsal, we are changing both our lives and the lives of our students in a positive way. If the beauty of the musical experience encourages vulnerability and the recognition of the shadow in our unconscious as well, the results are not only individual but spill over onto our students.

Is it then a special privilege to be a conductor of music? Obviously, yes, when you think of some of the problems we face today. If we accept the lifelong challenge to be a clear, effective channel for the great power of music to flow through to others—which is totally anti-negative and anti-judgmental—then we will produce **lasting** moments that "revive and readapt time and space." Both we and our students can experience a lasting inhalation of "the strange, special air" of music!

Lecture 3
Creating the Special World on a
Daily Basis: The Rehearsal

Not long ago your music students walked into your
rehearsal room, eagerly anticipating the prospects that
lay before them in the coming year. Their interest was at
a peak—their attitude most receptive. Among this enthusiastic group there may have been a few with some
doubts as to whether they were going to enjoy being in
this room working all year. Nevertheless, they were
there. The director assembled the group, and the first
rehearsal began.

It is at this moment that the conductor has within his
or her grasp a most splendid opportunity. The mind of
the student is at its most open and receptive state. The
impressions that enter their minds in the next thirty
minutes will be determining factors in the success of the
year that lies ahead.

What can you do as a conductor to ensure that
students leave this rehearsal thrilled with the prospects of
the forthcoming year? First of all, in a short, and I stress
short, talk, convey your genuine enthusiasm for the
potential of the group now before you, the special projects
and concerts that lie ahead in the coming months, and
your unbounded joy in again having the privilege to work

with this group. It must be genuine enthusiasm on your part. If not, your lack of sincerity will hinder your "spark" of enthusiasm from reaching the students. If you are not genuinely thrilled to be before them, look within—you may need to switch professions. If the challenge that confronts you is *not* one that stimulates your entire being to do the best job possible, then you are not fulfilling all the students have the right to expect of you.

After this short speech from the director, students will be more enthusiastic to begin the actual rehearsal of the music. What criteria did you use in selecting your first composition? Are they going to feel a degree of excitement in their first encounter? Might they comment as they leave the rehearsal: "That was 'cool'—I really liked it!"?

If they do, the first piece probably possessed a comfortable tessitura and approachable intervals, was quite rhythmical perhaps with some unison sections, and, most importantly, had a strong climactic moment. When you arrive, hold that moment of the climax, and allow them and yourself to be excited at the prospects of the year before them. Your second selection may be in a contrasting style or based on a song that is familiar, e.g. a folksong or an excerpt from a musical. Your goal in this rehearsal is not the degree of musical accomplishment, but creating a positive state of the mind in the student. Is a spark of enthusiasm perceptible? If so, you have set the stage for a successful new year for your choir!

How are you going to sustain this enthusiasm? The responsibility is about 90 percent yours! The success or failure of each rehearsal is largely due to the conductor and what he or she did that day. What factors are present in a successful rehearsal?

A carefully planned rehearsal is vital. Discipline problems will be minimized if students are engaged at all times. A warm-up, including stated technical goal(s), should last no longer than five minutes. Consider ending warm-ups in the same key as your beginning selection. In this way, the attitude that the rehearsal is already underway is enhanced.

Here again, what criteria determined your choice of which selection to rehearse first? Either of two criteria might be used. It may be a piece they know quite well, which can serve to center the concentration of the singer. A selection of greater difficulty might follow. Even with the more difficult piece, I would begin at a place that has a good chance of being performed successfully. Too difficult a spot might deflate them, and, thus, a degree of the momentum of the rehearsal is lost. I rarely start at the beginning of a composition. I prefer a place of total involvement with a degree of climax. In this way you are always approaching more difficult music from a positive encounter. If sight reading is part of your rehearsal, this can be a good moment to introduce an exercise. Your final selection should be lighter in mood, one they might hum as they leave the rehearsal room. They are already anticipating the next time choir meets!

In the first encounters of a new composition, I often use a neutral syllable, such as "day." Students are trying to sight read intervals, rhythms, and text. Simplify it with the use of a neutral syllable at first. The long "a" encourages a relaxed jaw with a dental consonant enhancing forward placement. The accompanist should play single parts only as needed, concentrating on the "whole" as much as possible.

I discourage students from presenting any problems to me before the rehearsal—only at the end.

As the rehearsal progresses, students' continued involvement is vital. To enhance this, I often ask a question of an individual immediately after stopping the choir. Their peers will center their attention on this individual, eager to hear the answer, and relieved not to be involved. Student participation remains even though not all are actively involved. I often give the student a choice of answers so as not to embarrass an individual. I want it to be a moment of affirmation, of encouragement, never negative!

Another vehicle for student involvement is requesting that an individual vocally demonstrate the passage before him or her. Choir members often need to hear the correct concept in addition to verbalization. A successful student model is more effective than a conductor presenting the same concept. A less gifted student might be encouraged to be so involved, but only if the conductor sings with them. This again is meant to be a moment of affirmation, not embarrassment. The same procedure can be used in asking an ensemble to demonstrate. The students learn by osmosis; the voice is saved from unnecessary fatigue; the ensemble is affirmed.

Conductors should be encouraged to vary their teaching methods. Students respond differently to different methodologies, and reaching all of the singers often requires a variety of approaches. Enter the three methods of teaching: cognitive, affective, and kinesthetic. I prefer to deal with these three approaches in a later lecture, even though they are a vital part of the psychology of rehearsing and creating the special world.

In the late twentieth century, leading music educators met at Tanglewood (summer home of the Boston Symphony) to discuss the status of music education in the United States. The formation of the Tanglewood Declaration was the result. Simply put, it stated that we must educate our singers as musicians and not exclusively as performers. Music performance must have a foundation of musical knowledge. Rehearsals must take on added depth through an understanding of style, culture, historical periods, different types of scales, and form.

Wisconsin Comprehensive Musicianship through Performance (CMP) underscores this philosophy with practical suggestions, such as: "Instead of writing rehearsal titles on the board, ask the ensemble to take out the piece that is in ABA form, or the one that's in triple meter, or the selection that's in the minor mode. If you have a piece in ABA form, have students point out various examples of ABA in the classroom."

Will Schmid of the CMP adds, "A great way to help students understand staggered imitative entries (fugues, motets, madrigals, etc.) is to ask them to write a round. The easiest type of round for a novice to write is a rhythmic round. All the students need to do is to write a rhythm and indicate with an asterisk when the next part comes in. If students enjoy writing rounds, the next step will be to introduce pitch."

Students can be involved in research on composers or librettists, or deepen their understanding of form. Go to the Internet. Contact living composers to understand the circumstances that brought about the writing of the composition. Do not turn out choral robots—turn out choral musicians!

Any choir encounters "slumps." One must understand the reason why this has occurred. Perhaps positive rehearsals have been emotionally demanding and a period of refilling or renewal has to take place. Perhaps circumstances outside the choir room are present, such as final examinations or an athletic contest. Then again, a certain selection may be rehearsed for too long a time, and it is time to move to another piece. Involve your choir officers and get their perception. Try to identify the factor involved in the slump, present the information to your students, remain positive in your rehearsal demeanor, and a change will take place.

Find the right balance in detailed rehearsal versus "broader strokes." Encourage students to have a pencil and to make notations as you direct them. This will serve as a reminder in future rehearsals. When you stop a choir to make suggestions, give them a maximum of three suggestions. More than that will not be productive.

Be contagious in your enthusiasm for the music. Do not be afraid to reflect this in your face and vocal inflection. Be an encourager—a positive motivator. Perhaps above all, students must know you care for them, that you are genuinely concerned as to their personal welfare as well as their musical progress.

May all of the above contribute to known and unknown moments of the "special world" encounters for students. May they encounter life-changing moments in their choral experiences!

Choral Pedagogy

Lecture 4
Three Methods of Teaching

If I were to ask choral teachers how they teach, the majority would answer: "I react to the moment and give instructions accordingly." That would have been my answer for many years. The following lecture was part of a workshop I presented one summer entitled *The Total Conductor*, concentrating on problems the conductor brings to the podium before ever giving the downbeat, thus negatively affecting the rehearsal. Serving on the staff of this workshop was Dr. Geoffrey Boers, director of choral activities, University of Washington. One day he approached me and said, "Weston, do you know how you rehearse?" My answer was an emphatic "no." "Let me show you how you rehearse. Come to my session this evening on the *Three Methods of Teaching*." With great anticipation I witnessed how effectively his methodology would result in the "inclusion" of every individual in a choir.

Cognitive Teaching

When a conductor teaches cognitively, he or she uses factual information to gain an intellectual under-standing. Problems such as intonation, precision, or vocal production are often addressed in a cognitive manner. Students know exactly what the conductor wants. Cognitive instructions are usually the quickest means of reaching a solution to a problem. Students are used to this approach because of the frequency with which it is encountered in other classes.

Cognitive teaching can sometimes lack inspiration, the desire to *want* to learn. The instructions can be easily forgotten if no relationship is established with other avenues of instruction. If only the technical part of music is stressed, the result can be less-musical singing. Yet there is a time and place for cognitive rehearsing. When a new piece of music is being introduced, dealing with accurate rhythms and pitches demands a degree of cognitive instruction. How can one teach sight reading other than through a cognitive approach? Teaching proper vocal production also employs cognitive aspects, but certainly not totally.

Affective Teaching

Affective teaching is rooted in the Baroque *Doctrine of Affections*, more commonly known as "word painting," a compositional technique to enhance the meaning of a word or phrase in a text. Affective rehearsing is most clearly defined as the use of imagination during the rehearsal. This rehearsal method delves into the subconscious realm through the use of visual images and metaphors. Attention is given to the spiritual attributes of a given selection. It frees the imagination! Singers are free to feel and imagine, and a more musical performance is the result. If the text is accompanied by an imaginary visualization in the mind of the performer, the expressive content of the music will dramatically increase.

When affective associations are made with the text, the choir will remember concepts far longer than they will with only cognitive instruction. Beginning and advanced students can immediately be on the same level affectively even though they differ greatly in their musical knowledge. To a beginner, a cognitive request can be confusing—an affective request is immediately clear.

In 1958 at the New York Philharmonic's Young People's Concerts, Leonard Bernstein said, "There's no limit to the different kinds of feelings music can make you have…every once in a while we have feelings so deep and so special that we have no words for them and that's where music is so marvelous; because music names them for us, only in notes instead of words." Where cognitive explanations fail—enter the somewhat limited but more effective use of the affective method. What colors might be used to paint a picture at this moment? How many people would be on stage at this moment? Describe the amount of lighting. What physical posture might the actor(s) be employing? What compositional technique is the composer using to enhance the text? What "word painting" comes forth? These are the kinds of questions that spark the affective side.

When a conductor asks a student for his or her interpretation it is important to remember that when the imagination is used, no answer is wrong. For that individual it is his or her personal response. While there may be degrees of more appropriate responses, one should never say "no" to an answer.

Too much attention to the expressive and emotional aspects of a selection may result in the neglect of certain cognitive basics. A teacher may be overemphasizing the affective elements to compensate for a lack of knowledge about which cognitive elements to address. **A basic cognitive understanding of the piece must be present before the affective approach is employed.** Then, and only then, will affective strategies achieve the maximum benefit. Since some students are not as intellectually oriented as others, visualization can be a more effective method of engaging their attention. By using this approach, the conductor may reach yet another group of students in the choir.

Conductors must remember this basic rule when employing the affective method of teaching—**never ask an affective question without knowing how to achieve the answer cognitively.** An affective question may result in a simple cognitive solution, such as whether the note is lengthened or shortened. Dr. Boers said, "If a student answers an affective question with insightful interpretation and then can say how this can be brought into being cognitively, *this is the ultimate in teaching.*" I have often seen a mundane rehearsal turned around by the appropriate affective question. Then not only the mind is involved, but the spirit enters the arena as well.

Affective teaching is daunting to many conductors. How can I know I am correct? Trust your intuitive imagination first of all. Second, don't be afraid if you know the question but not the answer. Students will surprise you with their answers.

The ultimate goal of affective teaching can best be summed up in this basic question: How can a choir sing with emotion in the tone? There is no cognitive answer; the only answer is **by the use of imagination!** Research can show the process employed in formulating an answer to a cognitive question, but how the use of imagination is realized is a complete mystery. It is one of the most unique gifts that humankind possesses!

Kinesthetic Teaching

The term *kinesthetics* as applied to music refers to a bodily response, a physical movement to music. It is a gift that is innate within us. Dalcroze saw physical response as the basis for music making. When music is kinesthetically felt, it is uniquely fulfilling. If a singer responds not only intellectually and imaginatively but also physically, the body becomes the instrument. Some students find their way into the music, not through the mind or the heart, but through the body.

To be creative in the use of kinesthetic teaching is an art. All teachers use it extensively in early childhood education, but we gradually diminish its importance, until eventually there is little or no kinesthetic teaching. This is unfortunate. Research has shown that the learning process can be shortened considerably when kinesthetic strategies are employed. Memorization comes much faster because of bodily association, and certain longer learning processes seem to be skipped.

An element of maturity must be present in a choir to use kinesthetic teaching effectively. Otherwise it can be distracting and non-productive. Hand motions to follow a phrase, tapping of rhythms on a body part, an upward circle to aid in vocal placement—any gesture that will enhance the direction you desire to achieve—all are effective kinesthetic tools. Brad Holmes, choral director at Millikin University, is a master in the use of kines-thetic teaching. A wonderful video *READY, SET, SING!* by Jeff Johnson (Santa Barbara Publishing) illustrates the use of kinesthetic strategies in teaching vocal techniques.

Rarely is one conductor equally comfortable in all three methods of teaching. Usually one comes easier than the others. For me, affective teaching is wonderfully satisfying, and the challenge then becomes to combine it with cognitive implementation. I have grown consider-ably in this area. Kinesthetic still remains a less comfortable technique for me personally.*

What is our challenge as conductors?—to strive for a balance in the use of the three methods of teaching. Then, and only then, will the individual learning styles of ALL students be accommodated!

[*Editor's note: I found this comment surprising given all the movement we did as part of Nordic rehearsals. I vividly remember Mr. Noble and any number of students waltzing across the front of our choir room as we worked to get our triple meter to "dance."]

Lecture 5
Auditions and Voice Placement

Auditions are the bedrock of your choral program. Decisions made at this time are permanent. The atmosphere in which those decisions are reached is vital as well. If the audition process is related to peers as a good experience, more students will be favorably disposed to participate. The reverse is also true.

Spring auditions are becoming more the norm as the computer allows more advanced planning for registration by your administration. In the initial audition, I favor hearing students in groups of four rather than individually. Less intimidation is present. The group first sings the chosen selection together, followed by each individual singing alone. I find "America" to be a satisfactory selection. For sopranos, use the key of either A-flat or G-flat major; for altos, E-flat or D-flat major; for tenors, G-flat major; for bass I, E-flat major; and for bass II, B-flat or A-flat major. At this point, basic tone quality and pitch are my primary points of evaluation. If I have an overabundance of women auditioning, I find it profitable to include basic sight reading as part of this audition.

For many students, one can determine positive or negative results immediately. Questionable students can be recalled. Should one have the luxury of too many positive ratings, a full recall can be initiated. Here the auditor can listen for vowels and their placement, a "break" in the voice, tone color, and memory for tonal patterns to determine the strength of the ear as well as basic musicianship.

For a more advanced level, one can choose to involve former members as well as potential members. This group should be heard not only on a more challenging prepared selection, but also on an eight-bar melodic folksong or hymn. Two contrasting selections can show different aspects with regard to the student's capability level. At this point, more careful attention should be given to pitch (feeling of thirds and sevenths), the blending quality of the voice as to smoothness of tone and size of tone, the feeling for a chord (play an open fifth and ask the student to sing what is missing), vibrato (above or below the pitch), and strength of personality. In most situations, the audition process ends at this point, but how does one determine where each singer will stand within the section? This may be determined after the choir is chosen, or it may be incorporated as the final step in the audition process (with great value, I might add).

Any member of a choir has experienced ease or difficulty when singing with a particular voice seated to the right or left, or both. Blending conflicts can produce vocal tension and result in choir being a less enjoyable experience. Conversely, well-matched voices may enhance the ease of singing, resulting in more frequent "special world" experiences. It is difficult to understand the methodology for determining the placement of voices in your choir from only a written description. Hearing numerous combinations of voices is the only way to make a decision, but what factors determine the best combination? Certain factors such as pitch are obvious, but other factors are more subjective and depend on the musical taste of the director. Howard Swan, the great choral lecturer, said the "inner ear" of each director is determined mainly by his or her college choral experience. It is not difficult to grasp the significance of that statement.

What ingredients determine blend between singers and the choir in totality? One must consider tone color, vibrato, pitch, physical height, size of tone, and rhythm. To evaluate the presence or absence of these factors the following general guidelines might be used.

Voice Placement Procedure

- Find two people who have a natural vocal blend and have them sing together. These voices are your model pair.
- Having established a model pair, bring in a third individual. This singer sings first to the left and then the right of the first singer. Each time only the first and third singers are performing. The same process is repeated with the second singer. This person may become the new first singer, be placed between the model pair, be the new third singer, or none of the above.
- When you have the best spot, have all three sing together and then bring in a fourth individual and go through the same procedure. Ideally, each singer should blend with both the person on the right and the left—not just one individual.
- After the entire section has been placed in order, you might try flip-flopping them in a mirror image and hearing the entire section just to check the blend both ways. Sometimes the result is surprising!

While the end result may not be perfect, the best possible placement can be achieved. Directors might be inclined to place like tone colors, vibratos, etc., together, yet the discovery that "opposites" work can be very exciting. A person with a darker color placed next to a person with a brighter color can produce a beautiful blend as each one compensates for the other's uniqueness. A "straight tone" voice can be placed next to a singer with a greater vibrato with the same positive result. A person with a marginal pitch problem placed with a brighter sound may correct the marginal pitch problem. Certain individuals just sing more slowly so placing two individuals together with this problem can result in a negative situation, but, again, opposites can be the solution.

In junior high, one can add another factor to blend—**discipline**. Do not ask for trouble by putting buddies together. When opposites in personalities find themselves sitting together and perhaps become the best friends, it can be very rewarding not only to the individuals concerned but to the director as well. Place a non-singer next to a singer, and experience a miracle for the non-singer! It is a mystery, the factor present in the voice of the singer that brings this about.

The director must trust his or her inner ear to know what is the best combination. If this process is part of the final audition, then the director must make the final decision. If this process is completed after the choir is established, allow the students to participate. The voice-matching procedure can be valuable in junior high, but must be done more frequently, as voices are constantly changing. It also produces positive results in an elementary school choir, actually in all age levels.

In a less advanced ensemble, the two strongest sight readers may find themselves placed together, but the director might want them to be placed separately in the section to help other weaker singers. In this case, a "two-platoon" system can be used: one for learning notes and a second for the best overall sound.

Standard seating arrangements can be found easily in most choral education method books. Figure 5.1A illustrates a less-common formation that requires some further comment. A director rarely gets too much alto sound, so the advantage of formation A for balance is apparent. In this formation, the altos serve as a sort of scrim for the sopranos, and the sopranos, in turn, do not feel as exposed and sing more freely. Basses singing behind the sopranos give them a strong sense of pitch with the root being present much of the time. Also, a soprano in front of another soprano is not only challenged to blend with the voice on each side but the voice in back as well. This arrangement produces a more homogenized, less "sectioned" sound.

A mixed seating arrangement provides a nice variety for the ensemble member. One procedure for achieving a mixed formation that takes advantage of voice placement is to first have the entire section present, i.e. both bass I and bass II. Then have the tallest person sing with each member of that section. When a blend results, the tallest person moves to the back row with the partner standing in row three. People with larger voices sing more freely in the back row. Continue to follow the same procedure, putting shorter singers with smaller voices in the front row. Once all your rows of basses are blended, have the pairs stand in various combinations. Let your ear determine the best resultant sound. Do this same procedure with all four sections. The final placement creates vertical rows of altos, basses, sopranos, and tenors. As Figure 5.1B demonstrates, mixed quartets are created across each of the four rows horizontally.

Space between singers is a basic rule of thumb! A crowded choir loses freedom of sound, blend, and even volume.

Figure 5.1 Two sample choir seating arrangements.

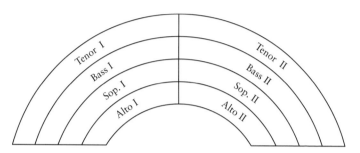

Figure 5.1A - Eight-part Choir

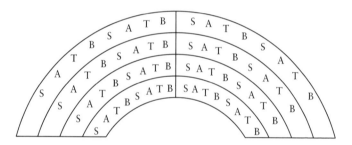

Figure 5.1B - Mixed

Lecture 6
Building Choral Tone:
Rhythm and Consonants

Rhythm

Rhythmic accuracy and stability must be the initial and most crucial rehearsal goal after that of "selling the selection." As Robert Shaw stated: "Rhythm is the bottom line of blend. If a choir does not arrive at the vowel together, how can you have blend?"

It has been stated that Mr. Shaw had "perfect rhythm" just as other musicians have "perfect pitch." I have known others with this rhythmic gift, but they are few and far between. Thus, the establishment of solid rhythmic accuracy is not an easy goal to realize. If the conductor is challenged to establish a stable rhythm, the choir can never achieve this basic fundamental.

How did Robert Shaw imbue this basic ingredient of rhythm in his choral music and musicians? Through the technique of count-singing. In count-singing, the pitches are sung on the note values and sub-divisions of the rhythm (one and two and three and four and). Anyone who had the privilege of singing under this great taskmaster knows how important he felt this technique was in establishing rhythmic accuracy. By including sub-divided beats in the counting, he ensured that singers internalized the feeling of the subdivision in the line,

49

another highly prized ingredient of the musicianship of the ensemble. The honesty with which conductors in his workshops had to face their own rhythmic integrity was challenging!

The degree to which Mr. Shaw pursued this technique is legendary. The moment the text was introduced, however, the effectiveness of this approach was vindicated beyond reproach. The choir was a unified rhythmic ensemble with the subdivisions being internalized to an amazing degree.

The timing of the introduction of count-singing is important. It should not be introduced until the notes are secure. The emotional content of the selection should have been experienced to insure the desire on the part of the singers to abandon the text for a period of time. Introduce it in a less-challenging part of the selection so that "success" is insured quickly. Block chordal sections with longer note-values are often a desirable starting point.

Counting can be counterproductive if a high tessitura is present. Mr. Shaw would encourage singing such a passage down an octave for vocal ease. For a less-advanced choir, it can be a real challenge to negotiate these quick changes in register without losing the pitch. With singers for whom the text is their "Linus blanket," counting is not a productive approach.

Employ the "oo" vowel before the word one to insure rhythmic sharpness (one and two and *tee* and). Also sound the word "three" as "tee" to achieve consonant sharpness. For a less-experienced group, count, but have two fingers touch the corners of the mouth. This will counter the tendency to spread the vowel (fish-mouth).

When the choir reverts back to the text, the sound will not be as pleasant. Initial consonants will be less rhythmic, and longer note values will be too lengthy. The degree of lip mobility can be less. An aid in making this transition would be to have the singers number off and split into two groups. Even-numbered members sing the text with odd-numbered members count-singing. The challenge will be for the even-numbered singers to keep up.

Junior high choir members can find this to be a positive technique if it is employed with a lesser degree of intensity. The non-reader may be learning the counting only by rote and with no degree of understanding, but this is true at any level.

Another technique to insure rhythmic accuracy is the use of the drumstick in rehearsals. As the choir sings on the text, have the drummer tap a subdivision of the beat such as the eighth- or sixteenth-note pulse. In a sense the drummer is doing the count-singing while the choir sings on the text. Since the first note we sing is almost invariably too long, have the drummer begin the subdivision tapping at least two beats before the choir enters. This allows the singers to internalize the tempo before a note is sung. The first note will be in rhythm with the entrance of the choir together, and the choral tone will be greatly improved. The rhythmic intensity of the entire phrase will be present. The ability to achieve consonant rhythm will be greatly enhanced. A neutral syllable accompanied by the drumstick can be used with great effectiveness rather than employing the full text immediately. The inner pulse of the line from the subdivision will establish basic musicianship. The choir will see immediate results. **All music must dance!**

Not every student can be given the responsibility of using the drumstick. Not every person can maintain a steady tempo. The temperament of the drummer should be one of calmness. Otherwise, nerves can be frayed by the constant repetition. Accompanists, too, will benefit from this approach. If the piano is heard in rhythm, the positive results for the singer are obvious. The conductor and the accompanist are now a team!

Other positive techniques in establishing a strong sense of rhythm are (1) placing your right arm on the shoulder of the person next to you and tapping the subdivision as the choir sings the phrase, (2) having singers tapping the subdivision on their own thighs, and (3) having each choir member conduct with a light snap of the finger.

The bottom line of blend is rhythm. How basic this is, yet how challenging it is to accomplish. "If you don't have rhythm in your group, you ain't got nuthin'!"

Consonants

When Fred Waring hired Robert Shaw to train his Glee Club in 1938, the future of American choral music changed forever. The repertoire a top-notch choir should sing, the standing arrangement to be used on stage (whoever heard of singing in a quartet formation?), a new concept of choral tone, the necessity of memorization, totally *a cappella* singing from the audience's perspective—all of these former concepts were challenged by this young, vibrant, gifted choral musician.

Prior to Robert Shaw, tone was based primarily on vowel uniformity, blending, model voice, and vowel modification in the St. Olaf tradition. Westminster Choir asked for "vitality of tone," a vibrant tone that was full, more weighty, and darker. The St. Olaf approach discouraged solo vibrato; the Westminster approach encouraged the natural vibrato. Yet we must remember Mr. Shaw was influenced and shaped by Mr. Waring. Fred's choral sound was all related to diction, where the text and sound of the word are of supreme importance. Splendid diction and excellent legato phrasing were hallmarks of the Fred Waring Glee Club. Every pulse of music must begin with the vowel sound. This necessitates the rhythmic placement of the consonant **before the beat.**

As young choral conductors heard this phrase **before the beat** it seemed revolutionary. Yet conductors had asked choirs to arrive at the vowel together for a relatively long time. I must admit I was puzzled for quite some time as to how one could be certain the consonant was being sung ahead of the beat. While listening to a King's College recording, I heard the sharp, short, crisp consonants. I knew I was hearing the correct interpretation of this consonant admonition. At that moment, I concluded that the singing of the consonant ahead of the beat is a psychological phenomena. You cannot measure it exactly, but the intent is there!

When asked at a workshop, "Mr. Shaw, how do you achieve blend?" I, as a participant, could not wait for his answer. After a pause, he said, "I achieve blend through **rhythm!**" I was crestfallen—rhythm? Then he went on to say, "You directors spend so much time trying to achieve vowel uniformity, and then you never arrive at the vowel together!" Consonants establish rhythm—vowels establish beauty of sound. "Do you directors know the three basic rules of consonants?" he asked. No one volunteered an answer.

The three fundamental rules of consonants are:

Rule #1: Be ahead of the beat (Fred Waring: "begin every pulse or beat of music with a vowel").

Rule #2: Make the consonant short and properly formed (just a crisp touch of the consonant).

Rule #3: The consonant must have the same pitch as the vowel that follows. (Fred Waring: "Accurate initial intonation will result if singers always think in advance the pitch of the first vowel and sing the preceding consonant on that pitch.")

To me, this underscores the importance of first considering the consonant technique and then the vowel unification. (See Figure 6.1.) Listed below are inherent strengths of choral musicianship if initial consonants and consonants before syllables are properly executed.

Figure 6.1 Effect of properly formed consonants on choral technique.

Precision—if Rule #1 is properly executed
Intonation—if Rule #3 is properly executed
Vowel Uniformity—assists in forward placement of vowel
Diction—clarity
Attacks and releases—avoid delayed attacks
Breath—conserves breath if properly formed
Legato line—through eliding
Enhances proper vocal production—forward placement
Vibrato—more controlled with strong focus
Lip mobility—forced lip action
Vitality to vowel—forwardness with energy and confidence

Madeline Marshall, the great teacher of diction, formerly of Juilliard, was a teacher of Robert Shaw as well as Fred Waring, both diction experts. For her, the eliding of consonants was of great importance. One takes the final consonant of a word or syllable and places it rhythmically on the vowel that follows or with the consonant that follows. This lengthens the rhythmical duration of the vowel even more, enhancing the beauty of the sound. "Rob us" would be pronounced "ro-bus." (See Figure 6.2.)

54

*Figure 6.2 Some examples of consonant elision
as recommended by Marshall.*

Text	Elided Pronunciation
Rob us	(ro-bus)
Rob them	(ro-buhthem)
Send it	(sen-dit)
Send them	(sen-duhthem)
If it	(Ih-fit)
Strife-borne	(stri-fuhborne)
Beg us	(be-gus)
Beg them	(be-guhthem)
Age of	(a-geof)
Judge me	(ju-dgeme)
Full of	(fu-lof)
For us	(fo-rus)
Miss it	(mi-sit)
Grant us	(gran-tus)

N's or M's	(think to the left)
Anointed	(ann-oin-ted)
Another	(ann-other)*
Be mine	(bemm-ine)*

Y and **W** at beginning of a
word, are consonants, at
the end of a word, vowels

*Intensify the closed consonant so that the dynamics do not
change in the line. Thus, the double N's and M's.

If producing an initial or final consonant produces
vocal problems in a part, just drop it. To sing a "gl" on
a high A is difficult. Let the lower voices sing the full
word and sopranos go right into the vowel. Certain
consonants or consonant combinations such as "l" or
"gl" can be problematic because of the length of time it
takes to sound them. One solution is to have half of the
singers substitute the longer voiced consonant with a
related unvoiced consonant. For example, the "gl" of

"Gloria" becomes "Kloria," and the initial "l" of "laudate" could be replaced with a "t" for "taudate." This produces a crisper attack without changing the overall impression of the consonant.

If a rest follows the final consonant of a word, release the consonant on the pulse of the rest. If the final note is a quarter note tied to an eighth, I still release the consonant on the pulse of the beat containing the tied note. Sir David Willcocks stresses placing the consonant on the rest following the tied note. This is an interesting difference in philosophy.

Lecture 7
Building Choral Tone: Vowels

If choral directors are asked the question "What is the basic ingredient of blend in choral tone?" the most frequent response is vowel unification. When Robert Shaw was asked this question in my presence, he startled choral directors with this statement: "The bottom line of blend is **rhythm!**" Then he went on to say, "You directors work so hard to unify the vowel and never arrive at the vowel together—how can you achieve blend?" Enter the three rules of properly formed consonants to insure arriving at the vowel together plus a uniform pitch! [*Editor's Note*: see Lecture 6.]

Consonants establish rhythm—vowels establish beauty of tone. Thus, both the length and the quality of the vowel are of utmost importance. Fred Waring stressed, "Every pulse of music must begin with a vowel sound." To achieve this, Robert Shaw emphasized that every initial consonant must occur before the beat. What is the "original sin" of the amateur vocalist? To close in on the vowel by anticipating the consonant that follows, shortening the length of the beauty of the vowel. Madeline Marshall, the great teacher of diction at Juilliard, encouraged eliding the final consonant of a word or syllable to the following word or syllable. With proper attention to the initial and final consonant of a word or syllable, the length of the beauty of the vowel sound is insured.

I remember the rehearsal when Mr. Shaw said, "Now sing on the vowel only—omit every consonant." It was mush! Then he said, "Sing on the vowel only, but precede each vowel with the consonant "n." The difference in sound and ease of execution was amazing! When an "n" precedes each vowel, what are the positive results? A legato line is developed. Placement is enhanced as the voice is "thrown" into the mask with resonance following. The sounding of the "n" helps to relax the jaw, the dropping of the jaw. A feeling of "deadness" can result. Openness, then, enhances the beauty of the vowel sound. Remember, however, that the "n" can be too long for the goal of achieving of real consonant rhythm. To further enhance the effectiveness of this procedure, ask members of the choir to write in the proper vowel sound(s) under each word from the vowel pyramid in Figure 7.1 plus the word illustration for each vowel sound; not only is there further improvement, but proper vocal technique is enhanced.

Our next admonition: Sing on the vowel again, but this time precede each vowel with the consonant "t." It is a different sensation. What are the advantages of the "t?" Its inherent shortness and rhythmical sharpness insure proper consonant execution. The "t" also gives the correct focus to the sound, thereby giving the vowel forward placement and immediate execution. The tongue is relaxed and lowered. The shortness of the consonant conserves breath. It is a positive factor in enhancing lip mobility. Also, the resulting shortness gives rhythmic confidence and thus greater precision. In essence, rhythm is established very clearly and effectively. The weaknesses of the "t" is in the lack of legato line. It doesn't alleviate jaw tension, nor does it help diminish the spreading of the vowels.

Figure 7.1 The vowel pyramid

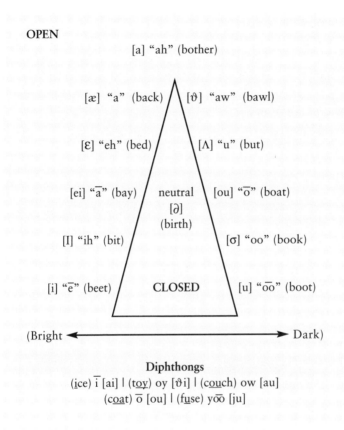

OPEN

[a] "ah" (bother)

[æ] "a" (back)   [ϑ] "aw" (bawl)

[ɛ] "eh" (bed)   [ʌ] "u" (but)

[ei] "a̅" (bay)   neutral   [ou] "o̅" (boat)
     [ə]
    (birth)

[I] "ih" (bit)   [σ] "oo" (book)

[i] "e̅" (beet)   **CLOSED**   [u] "o̅o̅" (boot)

(Bright ⟵⟶ Dark)

Diphthongs
(ice) i̅ [ai] | (toy) oy [ϑi] | (couch) ow [au]
(coat) o̅ [ou] | (fuse) yo̅o̅ [ju]

Using this same approach, have the choir precede each vowel with the consonant "l." Notice the relaxed dead jaw. Also notice the flat tongue. Place fingers in the hinge area of the jaw. Notice the enhanced legato line. The "l" does not aid in the shaping of the vowels. The effectiveness of the "l" lies in between the legato established by the "n" and the rhythmic sharpness established by the "t." As an interesting experiment, sing on the vowel preceded by a "y." Notice jaw relaxation.

Now have the singers number off and have every even-numbered singer sing on the vowel with a designated preceding consonant, and every odd-numbered singer sing the written initial consonant followed by the vowel. The challenge will be for the odd-numbered singer to keep up rhythmically!

Vowel Alignment

The need to keep vowels in line is not new to a student of voice. Working with vowel alignment in a voice studio by proper placement of each vowel is one thing; communicating this vital principle to a group of relatively untrained singers is quite another. The vowels need focus as they are often too spread, especially the brighter vowels. The following are suggestions to assist in vowel alignment in a rehearsal situation:

1. Have the "vowel pyramid" displayed prominently in the front of the choir room. Place one finger on the tip of the jaw. Sound the vowels on the ladder with as little jaw movement as possible.

2. Then place fingers one and three lightly on the corners of the mouth, and sing the vowels of the ladder or a phrase of the music. This is an excellent technique for vowel alignment!

3. Place the thumb and middle finger on the corners of the upper lip. Vibrate the upper lip whose corners were just touched. Notice how relaxed the upper jaw becomes. Again sing just vowels or a phrase.

4. We stress dropping the jaw so often that a conscientious student might well "lock" the lower jaw. Psychologically have them feel they are lifting the upper jaw. One might well couple this aid with number three.

5. A further aid to keeping vowels in line—precede each vowel in a vocalization with an "oo." Superb technique!

6. Whisper texts to get clearly formed consonants and vowels and to get lip mobility.

Below are suggestions to aid in vowel alignment for specific vowels:

1. "ee" vowel—pull in corners of the mouth (fish-mouth).
   a. five tone vocalization downward on "dickee, dickee, dickee, dickee, dee." Notice the forwardness, yet a touch of "ih" in the "ee" vowel.
   b. put an "oo" before the "ee" to get the right resultant sound.

2. "ah" vowel—tall vowel.
   a. five tone vocalization downward on "I-yi-I-yi-yah." Wonderfully dead jaw and forward placement but not spread. Incorporate exercise three from above with the same vocalise—wonderful feeling!

3. "oo" vowel—precede it with an "n."

4. "o" vowel—precede it with an "n."

5. "ay" vowel—five tone vocalization downward on "ee-ay-ee-ay-ee." Nice arch in the tongue. Diphthong is eliminated—pure "ay" with relaxed jaw.

6. "a" vowel (glad)—ugliest vowel we encounter as natural resonance of the throat is not present. Drop the jaw to open the throat.

7. "I" (ice)—Because of the diphthong, sound the "ah" component with greater emphasis—"AH-ee."

Three vowel fundamentals of which to be aware:

1. If the first vowel of a phrase is properly formed, the following vowels will have a tendency to stay in line until a breath is taken!

2. Students must have an aural concept of our instructions. Either the teacher must be able to demonstrate the above effectively or enlist the help of an outstanding student to demonstrate. Verbal instructions by themselves are not sufficient!

3. Voice placement within the section can aid the above immeasurably. Often a student with a bright tone sitting alongside a student with a "darker" tone will result in a positive combination for overall vowel sound.

Vowel Modulation

Vowel modulation is actually mixing another vowel sound into the basic vowel being sung, thus changing or altering the basic vowel to a certain degree by the entrance of the new "color." The use of vowel modulation allows the director to make suggestions for modifying or modulating the sound to attain uniformity and blend throughout the singer's range. One desires that sung vowels move smoothly from one to the next, vowel alignment being the result. A consistency of relative brightness or darkness can be attained. The following are general guidelines for vowel modulation (See Figure 7.2 for these rules in chart form):

1. To modulate "ee," mix "ih" or "oo." ("ih" is the next above on the vowel ladder). Basic problem of the "ee" vowel: too spread.

2. To modulate "ih," mix "ee" ("ee" is the next below on the vowel ladder). Basic problem of the "ih" vowel: too far back.

3. To modulate "o," mix "ah" (mixing "ah" makes it come out "aw," the next above on the vowel ladder). Basic problem of the "o" vowel: too far back.

4. To modulate "uh," mix "ah" ("ah" is the next above on the vowel ladder). Basic problem of the "uh" vowel: too far back.

5. To modulate "ay," just drop the jaw. This counters the tendency to go to the "ee" vowel too soon.

6. To modulate "oo," think "ee" ("ee" is directly across the bottom of the vowel ladder). Basic problem of the "oo" vowel: lacks animation and forwardness.

7. To modulate "a" (glad), mix "eh" ("eh" is the next below on the vowel ladder). Basic problem of the "a" vowel: too spread and bright.

8. To modulate "ah," mix "aw" ("aw" is two vowels down on the vowel ladder). Basic problem of the "ah" vowel: too bright and lack of depth.

9. To modulate aw, mix "ah" ("ah" is two vowels up on the vowel ladder). Basic problem of the "aw" vowel: too far back.

10. To modulate "eh," just drop the jaw. Basic problem of the "eh" vowel: too bright—lacks depth.

11. On any high "ee," "a," or "eh" vowel—think an umlaut formation. Assists in placing an arch or smile inside the mouth.

Figure 7.2 The vowel modulation chart.

BASIC VOWEL MIXING VOWEL
"ee" (see) "ih" or "oo"
"ih" (it) "ee"
"o" (for) "ah"
"ay" (may) drop jaw
"oo" (too) "ee"
"u" (but) "ah"
"a" (man) "eh"
"i" (ice) "ah"
"ah" (account) "aw"
"aw" (law) "ah"
"eh" (end) drop jaw

William Vennard explains vowel modulation in the following manner:

TENSE LAX VOWELS

Beat–bit: "ee" think "ih" Bait–bet: "ay" think "eh"
Boat–bought: "o" think "ah" Boot–put "oo" think "uh"

Vennard also says the order of vowels for a vocal exercise should be "ee-ay-ah-oh-oo."

Stylistic Awareness

Lecture 8
Stylistic Awareness in Renaissance Polyphony

In the middle to late 1950s, I was asked to be the choral clinician for the Iowa fall workshops. The requested topic for discussion was "Style Characteristics of Choral Music in the Different Periods of Music." I was reluctant to accept this invitation because I felt I did not know enough about the topic. From the 1930s until the late 1950s, tone was the single most discussed element of choral singing. The positive factors of this element were obvious, but the negative factor was obvious as well: all music had a tendency to sound the same with no differentiating characteristics of style.

I accepted the assignment with trepidation—this was my challenge to grow. With the help of the great Howard Swan, then at Occidental College in Los Angeles, I became the "style authority" for the state of Iowa! Our profession must have a stylistic awareness and a discriminating taste in directing choral music of various periods. As in the *Sound of Music*, let's start at the very beginning—polyphony.

Generalities

A study of music history shows us polyphony is the direct descendant of chant, and chant is the direct descendant of speech. Conclusion: speech and polyphony are thus closely allied. Each part must be heard when it presents important material. All parts cannot be preeminent at all times. Each melodic line is not of equal importance.

Specifics
Rhythm

Rhythm is present in Renaissance polyphony as in all music, but it is not metrical; it is not measured in the sense to which we have become accustomed through the use of bar lines. The rhythmic emphasis can begin any place within the phrase. James McKelvy's edition of *Gloria in Excelsis Deo* by Victoria (Figure 8.1, Mark Foster #404) is an outstanding illustration of the challenge of representing polyphony in modern notation. Here you see "phrases" that are four beats in length, two beats, five beats, etc. The beginning and ending of any segment of the rhythm is based totally on text. His addition of the bar lines makes the difference clear to those of us who have grown up with this basic principle of rhythm. Student comprehension is all but immediate. Yet, when sung, the melodic lines must sound as though there is no regard for bar lines. The music sets note lengths of melodic lines using changes of harmony, and this may or may **not** set **regular** measures.

Figure 8.1 The 1969 edition of Victoria's Gloria in Excelsis Deo
edited by James McKelvy

Remember my opening statement of polyphony being the direct descendant of chant and chant being the direct descendant of speech? Speech has a natural syllabic stress. This natural syllabic stress remains the same when set to music. The basic principle seems simple, but it actually is not. We naturally remain victims of the tyranny of the bar line—that beat one is automatically stressed if a modern edition of sixteenth-century choral music uses the bar line for clarity. Robert Shaw's 1953 edition of *O Magnum*

Mysterium by Victoria (Figure 8.2, G. Schirmer 43074c) is an excellent example of underscoring syllable stress yet using the clarity of the bar line. This was the first clear edition of sixteenth-century style that I encountered!

Figure 8.2 The 1953 edition of Victoria's O Magnum Mysterium *edited by Robert Shaw*

70

Figure 8.3 *The 1932 edition of Victoria's* O Magnum Mysterium *edited by John Finley Williamson*

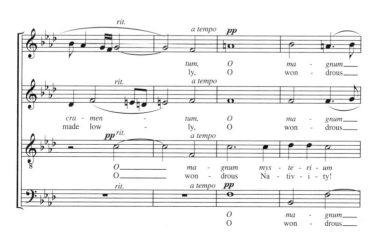

Melody

When notes of equal value proceed stepwise, they are nearly always sung legato. The larger the intervallic skip, the more the sensation of separation. Larger intervals often indicate word stress. The longer the note value, the more its intensity, weight, and body. Quick notes are taken lightly. If a note is tied over a bar line, there are no accents of any kind after the bar. Tension should appear in ascending lines, and relaxation in descending phrases. These are just the natural rules of speech.

Dynamics

Sing with good taste—**nothing** that smacks of effect. Great shades of dynamics are personal, as they are in the Romantic period. This, however, is group worship with the choir "leading" the congregation. The music must express the mood of the text, but not a personal, individual text—rather, a group text. Polyphonic composers often thought in terms of steadiness of sound with **the number of voice parts indicating the dynamics.** There must be an overall dynamic for the entire selection, centering on *mp* or *mf*, with little deviation for the entire number. A *crescendo* or *diminuendo* must not be obviously recognized as such, but as the intensity of small segments, the rise and fall of the melodic line. Imitative motives should always be recognizable, with more restraint on other parts rather than a harder pressing of the motive. It will be subtler this way.

Tempo

A fluent tempo is so important. Usually too slow a tempo is chosen, particularly in sacred selections. If a conductor errs on the slow side, he or she feels something is missing, and thus attempts to put in expression. This is wrong. Remember, pulse was the determinant, so the note values are relevant. Long notes are not sung more slowly just because they are long. Never take a composition at a faster tempo than the one that allows all details to be heard. Hans David, a great musicologist at the University of Michigan, said *rubato* could be used in polyphony so long as it is **within** the phrase and not **over** several measures.

Figure 8.4 The 1919 edition of Victoria's Vere Languores *edited by Kurt Schindler*

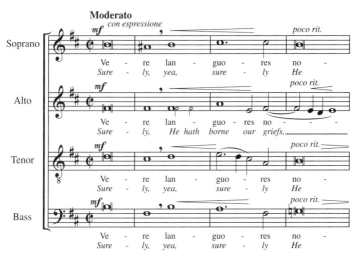

It is interesting to look at 1932 edition of *O Magnum Mysterium* by Victoria, edited by John Finley Williamson, formerly with the Westminster Choir (Figure 8.3, G. Schirmer 35752c) to see just how far we have come in critical stylistic awareness. Go to the 1919 edition of *Vere Languores* by Victoria, edited by Kurt Schindler (Figure 8.4, Oliver Ditson, No. 13,380). It is even a "dirtier edition," full of dynamic and tempo changes. Now refer back to James McKelvy's edition of *Gloria in Excelsis Deo* by Victoria. There is not one single dynamic marking or tempo alteration—it is totally clean! Bravo!

Lecture 9
Stylistic Awareness in Music of the Baroque

Generalities

As we enter the Baroque period (1600–1750), one does not find the one all-powerful Catholic church of the Renaissance. Instead, we encounter the strengthening of Lutheranism with the counter-reformation in Catholicism. The function of music within the two churches differed.

The Baroque period was primarily a revolt against elaborate counterpoint as composers wanted to get the words heard more plainly. Monteverdi's first opera employed the use of the solo song through recitation (prose rhythm of the text) and the aria (metrical organization). The recitation (recitative) fulfilled the great desire to project words clearly, interpreting primarily from the text; when an aria was performed, the interpretation came more from the musical connotation. True, there is counterpoint, particularly in Schütz and Bach, but it is more of a "throw-back" to what was prevalent before. Bach's sons did not view their father's compositions with unusual admiration; he was simply "behind the times."

We see a new emphasis on dramatic expressiveness as determined by the word. One cannot overlook the text in the Baroque, but it was not the structural element it was in polyphony or the emotional element of the Romantic. In this period, musical structure was determined more and more by harmonic implication. Thus, the change from Renaissance polyphony to the Baroque constituted one of the most drastic changes of emphasis in the history of music, second only to the revolution as we moved from impressionism to the twentieth century!

Specifics
Rhythm

Baroque music relies on meter. With the advent of the bar line at the close of the Renaissance period because of the complexity of the music, we find regular accentuations at regularly spaced intervals. Syllable stress was not the dominant factor in the establishment of rhythm. Rather than starting anywhere within the phrase, rhythm became very regular at regularly spaced intervals.

The advantages of metrical regularity also had a negative side. Beat one became so dominant as to take away a "dance feeling." The natural accents of a given measure gave a "square feeling" by nature of their undue importance. Duple rhythm especially could take on a pneumatic feeling of constant regularity.

Early in my musical career, I attended a wonderful Evensong at St. Mark's Episcopal Church in Seattle. As I congratulated Peter Hallock, he said simply: "Well, all music must dance!" I did not question him further, but I continued to reflect on his statement. A somber Lenten hymn must dance? A march? I understood how applicable this concept would be to triple meter, but duple?

Prior to meeting Hallock, I had spent two six-week sessions with Robert Shaw in San Diego. I recognized that he approached rhythm in a manner somewhat foreign to me. I felt the difference as we sang with him

76

day after day. I liked it, but what was the underlying principle—how could I verbalize it? His music danced! For him rhythm was not only timing, but spacing.

Several years later when sharing with an instrumental colleague, I mentioned how intrigued I was with the "Shaw feeling," but I found it so hard to verbalize. When I said I had never read anything about this type of phrasing, he replied: "Well, it is documented in a doctoral thesis at the Catholic University in Washington, D.C. Get a copy from their library." Soon I was reading *Note Grouping—A Method for Achieving Expression and Style in Musical Performance* by James Thurmond. I could not put it down. I had found gold. I knew the fundamental principle to make all music dance! The term "Baroque phrasing" became part of my musical vocabulary. I had a core curriculum of basic principles governing phrasing that prevailed at the time. And to my delight these principles prevailed in subsequent periods of music as well. I did not have to teach from intuition alone!

Baroque phrasing emphasizes what happens on the weak beats and between the beats, quite the opposite of the traditional concept of the dominating importance of primary accents (or natural accents) as customarily taught. Principal beats of the measure traditionally have been stressed through accents, a somewhat mechanical and unmusical technique. Rather, the principal beat should be approached from the previous weak beat!

Was this difference of approach the reason the performance of one artist touches our spirit so deeply while another may be technically intriguing but unable to touch a deeper side of ourselves? As James Thurmond studied in detail the note grouping principles of Marcel Tabuteau, the great oboist of the Philadelphia Orchestra, Baroque phrasing principles quickly emerged (weak to strong).

Nothing in life desires to remain weak if it is designated as such. Strength is the recognized virtue. Natural accents are obviously the strong beats of a given measure. Weak beats are inherently present as well. Can a weak beat become strong? If so, there are two possibilities for consideration, the strong beat before the weak beat, or the strong beat following the weak beat. It is impossible to look back and become strong, but one can look ahead and derive strength. Weak to strong is the underlying principle of Baroque phrasing! Interestingly, scripture states: "My grace is sufficient for you, for my strength is made perfect in weakness...For when I am weak, then I am strong." (2 Corinthians 12:9–10) Every weak note must never remain static but become strong by leading or "lifting" into the strong beat that follows. A weak note then becomes an upbeat!

> After much study of the extant literature regarding interpretation, expression and musicianship, it has been found that there is an important relation between the way the arsis (or upbeat) is played, and the movement imagery present in the mind when one is listening to music. This imagery of movement, as will be seen later, actually does affect the *kinesthetic* nerve system and can cause the foot to tap, or incite in one the desire to dance. How many times have we heard someone say, "What a moving performance!" or "I was so moved by his playing!"? The Reverend William J. Finn, director of the Paulist Choristers, was cognizant of this relationship when he wrote: "The mystery of music is in the upbeat." (Thurmond, pp. 18–19)

There are four basic rules in the accomplishment of Baroque phrasing that are applicable to all subsequent periods. Shaw added a fifth one, which I will explain later.

Rule # 1 – Weak to Strong

Any weak beat must lead to a strong beat. Nadia Boulanger, the great French teacher of so many of our great musicians such as Bernstein, Sessions, Copland, Barber, Menotti, etc., placed particular stress on the beat just before the bar line (e.g., four in duple meter). The weakest beat in any measure is just before the bar line. It must be lifted across the bar line to become strong with the energy of movement and flow of the phrase. Thus, the term "cross-bar phrasing" is also used in conjunction with Baroque phrasing. The tyranny of the bar line with undue emphasis on beat one must be overcome. As beat four must go to beat one, so must beat two (weak) lead to beat three. Triple meter is somewhat different and will be explained later.

Figure 9.1 Weak-to-strong phrasing for
quarter note rhythms in duple meter.

Square Phrasing   Baroque Phrasing

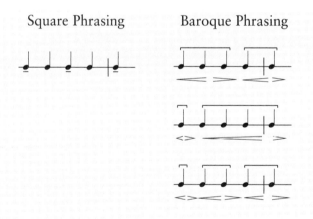

Two basic terms come into being, thesis (*thetic*) and arsis (*arsic*). Thesis in Greek means to fall, and is defined as a dominant point. Thus, all strong beats are termed *thetic*. Arsis in Greek does not mean "weak" as logic might indicate. Interestingly, it means to lift, to lead on to a destination—the weak beat leading on to the strong.

The same basic principle applies to shorter time values as well. When two eighth notes are present, the first one is the stronger, the second one the weaker. The destination of the weaker one is paramount. When four eighth notes are present, the first one is the strongest and the fourth one the weakest. In a faster tempo, rather than thinking the microcosm of the second eighth note going to the third (which it does) and the fourth going to the following note (which it does), one might feel the first eighth note as *thetic*, but the following eighth notes as *arsic*, all three leading on to the next downbeat. Tempo could be a determinant as well as the composer's preference.

Figure 9.2 Weak-to-strong phrasing for eighth note rhythms in duple meter.

Look at sixteenth notes. Most often the first sixteenth is *thetic* with the remaining three being *arsic* leading to the next downbeat. Yet in a subdivided passage, the second sixteenth might clearly go to the third one, and the fourth to the following downbeat. Again, tempo and the composer's taste become the determinants.

The function of a note might change. For example, if a measure consists of two half notes in 4/4 time, one might surmise both half notes are *thetic* in feeling. In this instance, however, the second half note is *arsic*, leading across the bar to the downbeat.

Figure 9.3 Weak-to-strong sixteenth notes in duple meter.

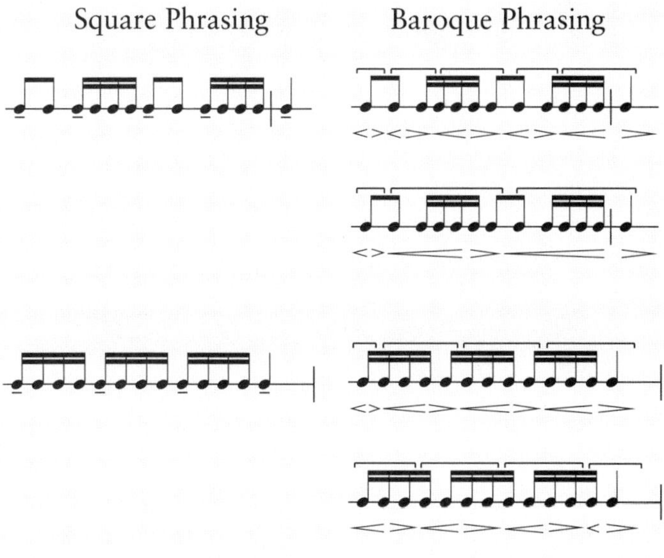

Square Phrasing   Baroque Phrasing

Rule #2 – Short to Long

Shorter time values always lead to longer time values. This is really a further clarification of Rule #1 in that the shorter time value is always weak, and the longer time value is always strong. Shorter time values can be viewed in two different ways. In the case of a quarter note followed by two eighths, followed by a quarter, the two eighths can be viewed collectively as weaker. The second perception of "short to long" is more obvious, such as a dotted quarter followed by an eighth. The eighth is the weaker and thus must lead on to the stronger beat that follows.

Figure 9.4 Short-to-long phrase groupings.

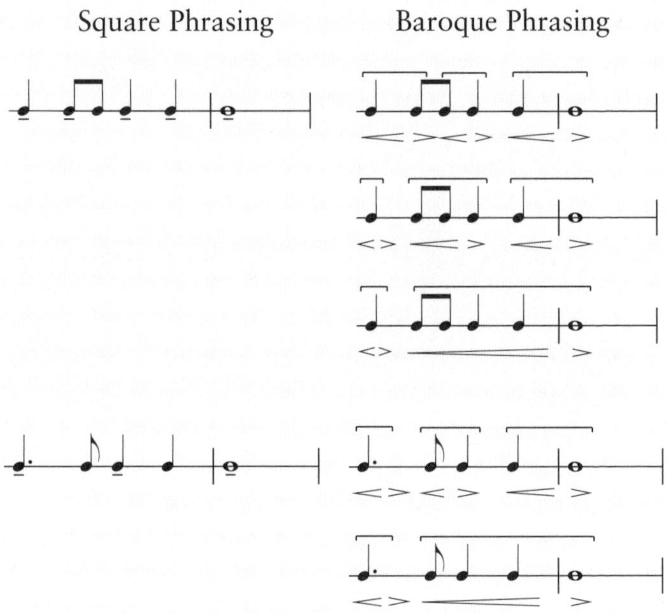

Square Phrasing   Baroque Phrasing

Now I want to introduce a term I use—springboard. Let us examine more closely the dot of the dotted quarter note. It is rhythmically an eighth note, making that eighth note *thetic* in relationship to the actual eighth note that follows. If it is viewed as *thetic*, it must have "energy," it must have strength, and it must have emphasis. It must function as a "springboard" to the eighth that follows. This can be realized by some emphasis being placed on the dot, especially by the conductor. In certain instances, Shaw would ask that an eighth rest be sounded on the

dot, or maybe a dotted sixteenth to give clarity of precision and emphasis, with the following eighth note leading
on to the next stronger beat. The same principle applies
to a dotted eighth followed by a sixteenth, etc.

Rule #3 – Repeated Notes

Repeated notes are often separated, again a further
subdivision of the basic "weak to strong" rule. As I
mentioned above, a shorter time value can be viewed as
a quarter note, followed by two eighth notes, followed
by a quarter. But much more often, the two repeated
notes have a feeling of separation. Shaw would state this
so elegantly, "Don't sing successive eighth notes as equal
values—sing the second one as a point of departure." If
two eighth notes are not thought of in this manner, the
tempo will invariably rush, and the intensity of the
phrase will be immediately be lessened in terms of its
forward motion.

Figure 9.5 Grouping repeated notes.

Rule #4 – Change of Song

If the melodic line changes direction, the melodic
turn determines the necessity of the notes after the turn
being treated as weak, with the note preceding the turn
being treated as strong or *thetic*. The following weak
notes are *arsic* in direction. If you look at the example
given after this explanation, it becomes immediately
clear how this enhances the flow of the phrase, as there
is a new burst of kinetic energy!

Figure 9.6 Change of song.

You can easily teach the above rules through the use of this simple poem:

Weak to strong, Short to long,
Repeated notes, Change of song.

Rule #5 – Just Because I Feel Like It!

Who else would dare add this rule! Think how deeply Shaw trusted his basic instinct—a challenge to all of us.

Now to triple meter. Baroque realization can be accomplished in two different ways, depending on the intent of the composer. It can be just beat three being led across to beat one with beat two being the realization of the downbeat (in other words, minimized), or it can be both beats two and three being led to beat one. The difference is quite stark and should be realized by determining the intent of the composer. The example in Figure 9.7 illustrates this.

Figure 9.7 Triple meter grouping.

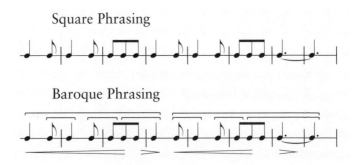

I explained my use of the term "springboard" in the "short to long" explanation. May I take this a bit further? Rests have a definite function in most instances. Visualize a 4/4 bar consisting of a quarter rest followed by three quarter notes. The rest is most often viewed as a moment of silence. This is wrong! The rest must be felt as *thetic*, with the following three quarter notes as *arsic* to the downbeat, or in a slower tempo; the first quarter note is *arsic*, leading to beat three, which would be *thetic*. In other words, the rest is a springboard, and the conductor must energize the downbeat to signal such. Otherwise, the first quarter note will always be felt as *thetic*, and this is absolutely wrong! Sometimes rests in the Romantic period are treated as moments of silence to enhance the drama of the moment. One must delineate between the two possible functions of rests.

What is the function of a tie? Just to lengthen the preceding note? Absolutely not! The second note of the tie must be viewed as a springboard as well, functioning as a *thetic* note, with the note following the tie being *arsic* in direction. The first note of the tie is *arsic*, leading to the strong beat second note of the tie. A static moment is avoided—the flow of the line is enhanced!

How does syncopation fit into this? One day in a rehearsal, Shaw pointedly asked me: "Weston, in syncopation do you feel the stress on the downbeat or the offbeat?" Flustered, I gave the answer, "The offbeat." "Wrong, Weston, you always feel the downbeat in syncopation to get the feeling of the offbeat." In other words, in syncopation you give the downbeat part of the syncopation a *thetic* feeling, which then gives the second part of the syncopation a energetic *arsic* feeling. Interestingly, in jazz it is just the opposite. I will never forget that moment with Shaw as long as I live!

How does one accomplish this realization of space between the *thetic* note and the following *arsic* note? The realization of this space results in the beginning of a new point of kinetic energy in the phrase, which is vital to fine music making. It is accomplished in two ways. The schism or indentation resulting in space may be an actual moment of space, which I term "sunlight." Or it may be accomplished in a mental sense, the resulting space being accomplished through "mist." The use of either depends on tempo, style, and degree of energy desired. I feel the most sensitive performer mentally lifts at moments, even if it is not directly indicated within the phrase. It is a wonderful constant subdivision!

Directors do not have time to explain every moment when Baroque phrasing is desired. It can be beyond the comprehension of the singers as well. If the instructor sings a passage with the desired result of this type of phrasing but substitutes a "day" for every *thetic* moment and a "tay" for every *arsic* moment, the choir will sing back what was emulated, and it will follow every basic rule of Baroque phrasing. And the music will immediately dance! The choir will respond with relative ease, simply because it feels so natural to be sung this way! One might use "du–tu–du" in passages that are quieter with less extreme ranges. A definite mood is realized, enhancing the beauty of the selection being learned. Recordings by the Swingle Singers are excellent examples of the use of syllables to enhance rhythmic groupings. Bach "swings" or dances as never before. Students are obviously drawn to this rhythmic feel.

Here are several rehearsal methods for gaining the feeling of a springboard: have the choir members tap on the dot, rest, tie, or downbeat syncopation, or the director may do the same. I often bob my head slightly, adding kinetic energy to the springboard. Shaw would often ask us to put a sixteenth rest within a dot or tie, creating space. This is particularly true in a larger ensemble.

Remember, all composers do not follow Baroque phrasing consistently. They may intentionally ask for a different phrasing to avoid monotony and to achieve individuality. One can trust the marking of Romantic composers in this regard. Prior to this period, the realization can be more complicated. In-depth study of the original score or style of the period are two factors that can help guide your decisions.

The above discussion deals with Baroque phrasing in the microcosm—one burst of kinetic energy to the next, arsis to thesis. Several microcosms put together can have an umbrella feeling of arsic or thetic. As more and more microcosms are put together, ultimately a musical phrase is the result.

The presence of a text gives singers a decided advantage in realizing the rules in our poem. Since articles and adjectives (usually weaker words) naturally lead to nouns, pronouns, and verbs (usually stronger words), a well-set text enhances the "weak to strong" principle. The string player also has a decided advantage since bowings are often determined by the "weak to strong" approach. Woe to the wind, keyboard, and percussion families—there are no built-in aids for you! It must be articulated.

I remember so well the day when I began to naturally follow the above rules to a certain degree. Understanding the rules thoroughly gave me a solid vehicle for teaching rather than having an ensemble mimic back what I either sang or instructed. Shaw gave us a new definition of rhythm. Rhythm is obviously timing, but now we must add the word SPACING! There is a world of difference! I end this section of Baroque characteristics with a Shaw quote: "Togetherness comes from a divided pulse—think sixteenth notes!"

Melody

Baroque melody asks us to think of chordal structure, harmonic in implication. Thus, the melody is generally in the soprano line rather than occurring in each voice.

Dynamics

Dynamics are most often terrace dynamics, not gradual changes from one level to the other. The same dynamic level is kept over a comparatively long period of time rather than changing abruptly. The effect of terrace dynamics usually comes about by the addition or subtraction of vocal parts or instrumental groupings. Bach added or subtracted from both vocal and instrumental parts in that he thought of both of these as one. Also no great dynamic ranges are called for. Many are aware of the group Mannheim Steamroller. Johann Stamitz in 1749 invented the orchestral crescendo with the Mannheim, Germany, orchestra. It was called the Mannheim crescendo, which, to Chip Davis, sounded like a Mannheim steamroller!

Tempo

Baroque tempos are unhurried, with animation but without haste. Tempos are even more regular in late Baroque, never exaggerated. Use rubato only with great discretion, not nearly as often as within Renaissance phrases.

Notes on Baroque Phrasing:

Thurmond's thesis has since been published as a text entitled *Note Grouping: A Method for Achieving Expression and Style in Musical Performance* (Meredith Music Publishing).

The examples in the figures were originally provided through the courtesy of James E. Richards, retired professor, University of Texas at Arlington. Notice the dynamic markings under the examples.

Suggested octavos for illustrations of the above principles:

Syncopation: *Jubilate Deo* by Althouse
  (Shawnee Press, A 1835)
Rests, dots, ties: *May You Be Led by the Highest Star*
  by C. Nygard (Hinshaw, HMC 1530)
Triple meter: *Summer Is A-Coming In*
  arranged by M. Braz (Hinshaw, HMC 1489)

Addendum: Stylistic Awareness in Music of the Classical Period

Generalities

The first generality of the Classical period is an absence of the "sweep" of the Baroque era. Instead, we find more of elegance in the music, a charm and grace. This brings into being the second generality: Onc always uses a lighter beat. Third, the structural perfection of the figured bass disappears; fourth, one finds a harmonic approach basically, with some contrapuntal harmony; and last, there is increased employment in the use of chromaticism.

Specifics
Rhythm

Composers begin to strive for unusual rhythms. One finds multiple meters not always indicated in the time signature. Also present are rhythmic alterations with dislocated natural accents, commonly known as syncopation. Composers have a desire for rhythmic surprises. (Haydn!) Also we find rhythmic energy even in rests. Therefore, the purpose of the climax determines the length of the rest. It must be determined by the emotion of the moment.

Melody

Longer phrases arise in the Classical period. Obvious cadences may often be avoided or resolved by deceptive cadences. Composers also strive to bring out color points in chords. Many interpretive markings are present, which are of great assistance. Without question, the melodic line is of utmost importance.

Dynamics

All dynamic devices are heightened even more. A true "orchestral crescendo" enters the music world.

Tempo

Tempos move more to the extremes—slower *largos* and faster *allegros*. We have more *accelerandos* and *ritardandos*. One finds more sudden stops and starts.

Choral Music:
A Retrospective

Lecture 10
Choral Music:
Past, Present, and Future

We are members of a very young profession. How young? The roots were just being established when I was born, and that was in 1922. I am defining choral music in this context as *a cappella* singing in the United States. Singing societies have existed since the beginning of our country, but the history of *a cappella* singing in the United States has occurred within my lifetime. Yes, we are a young profession!

By the mid-1850s, most of North America's large urban areas were home to at least several large oratorio choruses. Among the earliest of these choirs were the Handel and Haydn Society of Boston founded in 1815, the Mendelssohn Glee Club in New York founded in 1873, and the Apollo Club in Chicago established in 1871. Similar organizations were founded in many Canadian cities as well.

Prior to 1850, the largest group of immigrants to settle in the United States and Canada had been from England. After 1850, however, millions of Germans, Scandinavians, Italians, and Eastern Europeans settled on North American soil. These shifting patterns of immigration had a profound effect upon the evolution of choral music in North America. Germans in particular considered amateur singing societies a vital part of their cultural heritage, and the Scandinavian heritage was furthered by similar singing societies. Of particular interest to me is the Luren Singing Society in Decorah, Iowa, founded in 1868, which is at its highest artistic peak at the present time. In the late nineteenth century, no fewer than four other Norwegian singing organizations were present in the same county!

Another significant trend shaping North American choral music in the nineteenth and twentieth centuries has been the establishment of choral music programs at colleges and universities. In 1808, a male glee club was founded at Harvard University, followed by Yale in 1812. By the latter part of the nineteenth century, most colleges and universities throughout North America had some form of choral organization on campus. The goal of many of these collegiate ensembles, however, was entertainment.

A notable beginning for the *a cappella* choral tradition occurred in 1913 when the St. Olaf Choir under the direction of F. Melius Christiansen (a former band director) embarked on a tour to Europe. World War I intervened. Then, in 1920, they gained the attention of the choral world in the U.S. on a tour to the East Coast, filling the Metropolitan Opera House! Indeed, the *a cappella* tradition was born.

The second college mixed choir that was especially influential upon choral singing in North America before World War II was the Westminster Choir directed by John Finley Williamson. While Christiansen and Williamson differed greatly in their concepts of the ideal choral tone, each conductor was well known and highly respected for the performance standards attained by his ensemble. The repertoire of both choirs was kept purposely quite small, so that there was sufficient rehearsal time to resolve and polish every nuance prior to performance. The annual St. Olaf repertoire consisted of no more than twenty-five unaccompanied selections, despite the fact that the choir rehearsed at least ten hours each week. Peter Lutkin, then at Northwestern University in Evanston, Illinois, also helped pioneer this new venture. The major tenets of this new tradition were in place, and I was only four years old! Lurking in the background at this time (1922) was a young gentleman named Fred Waring, who had a singing band. But more about that later.

These new *a cappella* choirs had to have literature to perform. From 1920 to 1930, the literature for this genre had to be rediscovered or composed. F. Melius Christiansen wrote music for the St. Olaf Choir. John Finley Williamson edited choral masterpieces from the past. Other choral musicians entered the scene and made their unique contributions.

What new choral techniques had to be learned to have an *a cappella* choir that could sing in tune? From 1930 to 1940, choral musicians concentrated on developing choral techniques and conducting techniques. Two predominant schools of thought came into being—the individual being subjugated as part of the whole, or the individual remaining as an individual yet part of the whole. The first concept made ensemble blend of primary importance, the second made the individual singer the most important while remaining part of the whole ensemble. Choir schools were established by both Christiansen and Williamson, who put their individual stamps upon this new profession.

While Christiansen was the champion of unaccompanied singing and straight tone (non-vibrato) sound, Williamson favored a more deep-throated tone that tended to give a baritone quality to the tenors and an alto quality to the sopranos. Especially during the 1930s

95

and 1940s, choral directors throughout the continent continually debated the merits and shortcomings of the St. Olaf and Westminster approaches to choral tone and vocal pedagogy. Ultimately, both tonal concepts became equally controversial in the eyes of most American choral directors and voice teachers. The dedication, precision, and care with which Christiansen and Williamson both approached their choral work did have a positive impact on choral performance, however. Virtually every type of choral ensemble in America began to think about the importance of tone quality and vocal production in successful choral performance.

National contests spread an awareness of *a cappella* singing in the late 1920s and 1930s, with choral music growing considerably in the public schools. I was part of this scene. Interestingly, at this time we were already twenty years behind the instrumentalists!

Earlier I mentioned Fred Waring. His influence as a conductor grew as his "singing band" began to appear on national radio. I was drawn to a program called *Fred Waring and His Pennsylvanians*. Nothing motivated me more to get my chores done than to be able to listen to Jack Armstrong, *The All American Boy*, *Little Orphan Annie*, *Amos and Andy*, and Fred Waring. In 1939, he established the Fred Waring Glee Club separate from his band and hired an unknown college graduate to be the director of his new ensemble—Robert Shaw! I was then only sixteen years old and in my most formative years.

From 1938–39, when I was in high school, Sunday afternoons were the high point of my week. I would listen to the New York Philharmonic, often joined by the Westminster Choir. Each weeknight I would revel in the sound of Fred Waring and the Pennsylvanians. I had an awareness of the St. Olaf Choir. My inner "choral ear" was being formed.

When I was in college at Luther, not only were the above influences prevalent, but I heard the St. Olaf Choir for the first time. At the same time, Robert Shaw was conducting the Fred Waring Glee Club, and a national men's chorus contest was sponsored by Fred Waring. Lara Hoggard, then at Oklahoma City University, was the winner!

After World War II, there was a wonderful resurgence of enthusiasm for everything, including choral singing. Men returned to college campuses with a new maturity of sound. In 1949 Paul Christiansen dared to take the Concordia Choir on a tour of Norway, which was an overwhelming success. St. Olaf resumed coast-to-coast tours. The Westminster Choir would tour around the world. In the fall of 1948, I attended a concert on the first tour of the Robert Shaw Chorale. I had never heard anything like it; they even sang the Poulenc Mass in G.

Again my inner choral ear was being bombarded with different sounds—the tone syllables and the resultant Waring sound—the choral philosophy of the Lutheran touring choirs of which I was about to be a part—and the wonderful sense of rhythm as portrayed by Robert Shaw! Which won out? You answer that.

We began to see a proliferation of choral/conducting technique workshops. Robert Shaw established a six-week residency with the San Diego Symphony with the choral participants being his choir. (I attended two of these.) Paul Christiansen spent his summers going from one workshop to the next. Fred Waring did the same at Shawnee on Delaware. Williamson (and his students) "invaded" Texas. In 1957, I was asked to do two workshops for Iowa choral conductors on style. What a challenge! No one was talking about style with the same passion as technique. I really had to do my homework. Thank you, Howard Swan!

Los Angeles became a Mecca for choral music with the incredible influences of Howard Swan at Occidental College, of Charles Hirt at USC, and of Roger Wagner and the touring Roger Wagner Chorale. The Robert Shaw and Roger Wagner Chorales began to change the college and high school director's image of what repertoire a top-notch choir should sing, how they should be arranged on stage (e.g. quartets, spacing), whether memorization was essential, and whether an entirely unaccompanied program was indeed the most satisfying for an audience.

Colleges and universities were establishing reputable advanced degree programs. Among the first collegiate institutions to establish advanced graduate programs in choral music were the University of Illinois, the University of Southern California, and the University of Colorado. One could now get a doctorate in choral music. Music camps sprouted up all over the United States on college and university campuses. Lutheran choirs toured with vigor; Concordia was even gone for three weeks! All-State Festivals, Tri-State at Enid, Oklahoma, the Buccaneer Music Festival, Six Flags, the Greater Southwest—all enhanced our growing profession.

Authentic editions of sixteenth-century music began to appear, the most notable for me being the Robert Shaw edition of *O Magnum Mysterium* by Victoria. Paul Salamunovich became the "bishop of chant" to the delight of us all, and his resultant influence on the performance of sixteenth-century choral music was significant. Roger Wagner became a model for us on his coast-to-coast tours.

Enter ACDA and I, as a charter member in my eleventh year (1959) of college teaching. The uniquely vigorous ICDA came into existence. Conventions and workshops became the "order of the day." We were young, but we were growing tremendously as a profession. We even dared to hold our own first national convention! The goal for so many college music majors was to be the finest choral director possible.

Then came the explosion of the 1970s. Robert Shaw was touring with the B Minor Mass; we saw the phenomena of a men's ensemble as evidenced by the King Singers, later Chanticleer, and today Cantus; and the birth of a genre with elements of a show-choir/jazz-choir at Iowa Central Community College in Ft. Dodge, Iowa, in 1972 under Gene McKinley. How young are we? A young choral conductor in Owatonna, Minnesota, who became the National Teacher of the Year decided to form a choir of adults from his area, and the Roger Tenney Chorale was born. How many like ensembles have we seen spring up all over the country, fulfilling the dreams of every music educator that music continue into adult life? Dale Warland established a professional choir in Minneapolis, Minnesota. Margaret Hillis was asked to establish a chorus for the Chicago Symphony. Now an organization exists for these choirs called Chorus America. The Norman Luboff Choir went on tour for months at a time with the unique blend of the classical and the popular. Norman Luboff's gracious widow now heads Walton Music. Again, see how young our profession truly is!

How well I remember the ACDA National Convention in San Antonio, hearing the Toronto Children's Choir under the direction of Jean Ashworth Bartle sing *Bist du bei mir* by Bach! Children's choirs are the latest phenomena; enter Henry Leck and the Indianapolis Children's Choir, Doreen Rao and the Glenn Ellyn Choir, and James Litton and the American Boy Choir!

Graduate degrees are now mandatory for advancement in our profession. Fine doctoral programs are in place at many leading universities. We have seen a decline in music camps as our youth begin working in their spare time as never before. Slowly, we see more students majoring in vocal performance rather than almost exclusively music education. How this has grown! Professional organizations now offer to take our choirs to any place in the world for a festival— especially in the Western Hemisphere.

Out of Sweden came a name and a choir to become a new model for the choral world—Eric Erickson and the Swedish Radio Choir. Their appearance at the National ACDA in Nashville was a historic event. As northern Europe (Leipzig in particular) affected the St. Olaf Choir, now northern Europe is exerting its influence once again.

Moving into the later 1980s and 1990s, Robert Shaw continued his influence from Atlanta and France with memorable recordings coming into our homes via CDs. We notice a change in choral tone. At one time, Shaw is believed to have said, "My idea of a choir would be singers from the Metropolitan Opera." Now American choirs participate in and win European choral festivals. An influence is inevitable. The Westminster Choir sound changed under Joe Flummerfelt and the St. Olaf Choir changed first under Kenneth Jennings and then Anton Armstrong. The center of choral music moved from Los Angeles to Minneapolis/St.Paul. Helmuth Rilling extended his influence through the Oregon Bach Festival, a new major European influence. Tallinn, Estonia, continues to astound the choral world, through director Tõnu Kaljuste, as does Finland. Korea has emerged as a choral center to rival Sweden, some say even to overtake it. The International Federation of Choral Musicians has come into being with international conventions every three years. Choirs from Mongolia and Cuba stun us with their artistry.

The death of Shaw in 1999 left a vacuum. Our hero is gone, and we all need a hero. Erickson, although retired, continues his work, but more in Europe than in the United States. Helmuth Rilling will continue his great work in Oregon and all over the world. Sir David Wilcocks and John Nelson will be busier than ever, if that is possible. It is fascinating to see new young stars emerging throughout the country to become our future leaders (e.g., Charles Bruffy in Kansas City). High school students are entering college with a level of training that I hope will become only higher in succeeding years.

The availability of the Internet to disseminate information, the great quality of fine recordings available as learning tools, and great performances on television all contribute to an explosion of knowledge. Diversity is the word for today. The world gets smaller year by year and with it the choral world. As we of the West meet those of the East, more and more through travel, recordings, and IFCM, and as the East comes to meet the West with greater frequency, influences are inevitable. This produces growth. Now the question for me in the new millennium is will the East influence the West more, or the West the East? Europe or the United States? I have my opinion. What is yours?

Recommended Recordings and Resources

Evocation of the Spirit by Robert Shaw.

Kaptein, Lawrence. 1988. "Three-and-a-half Centuries of Choral Singing in North America,"
    International Choral Bulletin, vol. 8, no. 2.

The Legacy of F. M. Christiansen by the St. Olaf Choir.

Recording from the book *Fred Waring and the Pennsylvanians*.

Recording of Bach by Robert Shaw early in his career.

Sounds of the First 50 Years by the Westminster Choir.

About the Author

Weston H. Noble is director of music activities at Luther College, where he conducts the Nordic Choir. He is an internationally known conductor and clinician and has served as a guest conductor for more than 775 music festivals in the United States and abroad.

Noble received the first Outstanding Music Educator Award from the National Federation of High School Associations in recognition of his contributions to the quality of performance in high school music programs. He has also received the Iowa Music Educators Association Outstanding Music Educator Award, the Illinois Music Educator Association's Presidential Award, and the Citation of Merit Award from the University of Michigan.

Noble holds a bachelor of arts from Luther College, a master of music from the University of Michigan, and honorary doctorates from Augustana College and St. Olaf College. In 1998, he was awarded the St. Olaf Medallion by King Harald of Norway.

He is a charter member of the American Choral Directors Association and an elected member of the American Bandmasters Association.